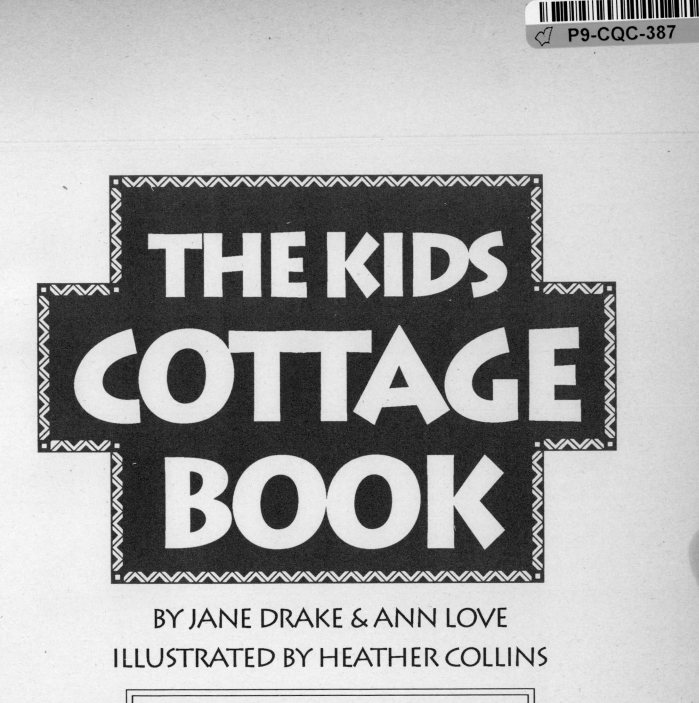

THE KIDS COTTAGE BOOK

BY JANE DRAKE & ANN LOVE

ILLUSTRATED BY HEATHER COLLINS

KIDS CAN PRESS LTD., TORONTO

Canadian Cataloguing in Publication Data

Drake, Jane
      The kids cottage book

Includes index.
ISBN 1-55074-132-2

1. Outdoor recreation for children. 2. Amusements.
I. Love, Ann. II. Collins, Heather. III. Title.

GV1203.D73 1993 j790.1'922   C92-095165-1

Kids Can Press Ltd.
29 Birch Avenue
Toronto, Ontario, Canada
M4V 1E2

Edited by Laurie Wark
Designed by Blair Kerrigan/Glyphics

Printed and bound in Canada
by Gagné Book Manufacturers

⚛ Text stock contains over 50% recycled paper

93 0 9 8 7 6 5 4 3 2 1

This book is dedicated to

**Jim, Stephanie, Brian, Madeline
&
David, Melanie, Jennifer, Adrian**

*with whom we have loved and savoured
many happy, crazy and active
summer days.
We're looking forward to
many more to come.*

CONTENTS

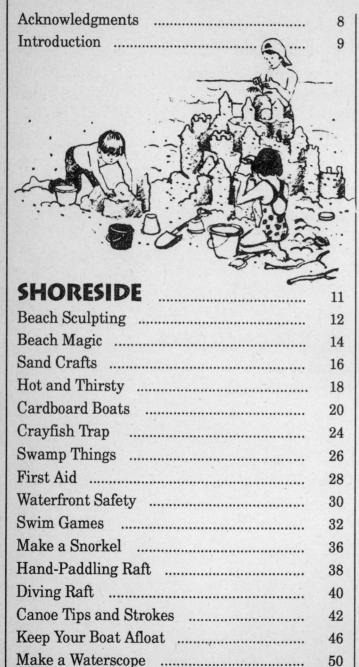

ACKNOWLEDGMENTS

The authors acknowledge the contribution to this book of the following people:
Andrea, Brianna, Natalie and Hilary Barnett and their family at Shuswap Lake; Greg and Patrick Barnett and their parents; Kathleen and Henry Barnett and every kid who loves Pipsissewoods; Donna Bennett; Cathi Bremner; Jack Brickenden; Jessica Bartram and her parents; Saran Bickram; Nellie Chisholm; Kathy and Bob Clay; Jane Crist; Kurt Crist; Mary Dobson; Chris and Mike Drake; Mary Beth Drake; Ruth and Charlie Drake and all their grandchildren at Lion's Head; Irmgardt Duley; Jane Falconi; Alan Foster; Jennie Gruss; Sara Irwin; Donald and Kathleen Leitch; Geoff and Ben Lewis and their parents; Matthew Litvak; Betty and Gage Love and all the warm fun at Westwinds and Windgage; Melanie Manchee and her whole clan; Carolyn Marshall; Kim, Brett, Janine and Sean Passi; Mary Jean Potter; Steve and Maria Price; Hilary Robinson; Ian Sedgwick who loved the cold water of Georgian Bay; Yvonne and Jack Sellars; Stephanie Smith; Dennis Stitt; Malcolm Sweeny and his Muskoka roots; Mary and Ron Tasker; Andrew, Mary and Doug Thompson; Douglas Wright and Val Wyatt.

We couldn't have written this book without old and warm summer memories with Jim Baillie, Barb and Vic Barnett, Doreen Barnett, Sadie and Thomas Barnett, Bill and Peggy Clarke, Muriel Flavelle, Tony and Mary Franks, Millie and Thomas Gourlay, Kit and Murray MacDonald, Ed and Marg McClure, all the Morgans, Anne and Bron Robinson, the Spitlers, Anne and Duncan Smith, Bob and Kay Taylor and Madeline Woolatt.

Thank you to Valerie Hussey, Ricky Englander and all the people at Kids Can Press. It's been a great pleasure working with illustrator Heather Collins and book designer Blair Kerrigan. A special thank you to editor, Laurie Wark, a fellow cottager. She enthusiastically welcomed all ideas — traditional and unconventional and helped us fit as much as possible into 208 pages!

INTRODUCTION

You may spend the summer at a lake or a river, at a farm or by the sea. Wherever you go, there are things to do. This book is full of ideas to add sparkle to your summer. Whether you're on the shore or in the water, out after dark, hiking, camping, or inside because the weather's rotten, just flip the pages to find ways of turning an ordinary summer's day into a great one. And if it's one of those days when there's just nothing to do, browse through and find easy instructions for lots of exciting new activities.

For instance, have you considered erecting a flagpole or sewing a hammock? You could track animal prowlers, catch a meteor shower, learn paddling strokes or call a loon. What about preparing wild snacks or modelling a clay spider? Maybe you'd rather feed summer birds, build a bat box or spy on moths. You might even do a snake survey, identify fossils, make monster bubbles or a variety of these all mixed together.

Most activities can be done with materials found around the cottage — some need an adult helper. Choose what you want to do, round up your materials and get started.

SHORESIDE

Head down to the shore, where land and water meet, and you'll find lots to do. The beach is a great place to make sand castles or sculptures, launch toy boats, check out creatures in the shallows or practise water tricks. When you get too hot, it's easy to cool off by jumping into the water. Why not try out a fun new swimming game while you're there? Or maybe you'd like to make a snorkel, practise the J-stroke in a canoe or dive off your home-made raft? There's lots to do when you leap from the hot shore into the water.

BEACH SCULPTING

This summer, try to build the biggest and most elaborate sand castle ever. The Guinness World Book record for the tallest castle is 5.94 m (19 feet 6 inches) high. Can you beat that? Here are some ideas to get you started on your castle creations.

PREPARING FOR THE CASTLE CHALLENGE

Get ready to build your gigantic sand castle by gathering as many different sizes of plastic containers as you can. Look for empty yoghurt cups, ice-cream and margarine containers, flower pots, even a toothpaste lid. Jelly moulds, cookie cutters, pot lids and spring-form pans will make unusual shapes. (Check with an adult before taking kitchen things to the beach.) An empty plastic pop bottle, with the top part cut off, will give you a pail with a fancy design on the bottom. Empty clam shells can be packed with sand and inverted. For massive undertakings, you might want a shovel or other garden tools. You'll also need a Popsicle stick or a smooth piece of driftwood to round out the contours of your creations.

The best sand castles are made with moist but not sloppy sand. Make sure you pack the containers well before turning them upside-down. If the sand is sticking to the pail, squeeze the top of the container to loosen the edges.

GOING FOR THE GUINNESS RECORD

1.
Start with your largest container to make the foundations and walls. Then use the smaller containers to add character to your creation. If the sand is wet enough, you'll be able to fill the pop bottle, invert it on the castle and create turrets.

2.
Finishing touches can be made with pine cones, bird feathers, sticks, shells, smooth beach glass, driftwood, stones or anything else you find beachcombing.

3.
If you've got a friend on the beach, work together to make a huge, connecting town. Be sure to collect all of your containers and tools when you're finished building.

SCULPTURES

Sand sculptures are easy to make using your hands and a shovel. Mound moist sand into the desired shape, packing the sand firmly with your hands. Your own creative genius will tell you what you can sculpt in the sand, but here are a few suggestions to get you started.

DRIBBLE CASTLES

Sit at the edge of the water where the sand is wet—just beyond the reach of the waves. Take a large handful or pailful of dripping sand. Let it slowly dribble into a pile. Create your own lumpy, swirly structure, moving in a circular motion. It won't look like a conventional castle, but it will look great when it dries. Don't forget to keep the sand really wet while you're working with it.

SAND DINOSAURS

Recreate the Mesozoic era (the age of the dinosaurs) complete with prehistoric creatures. *Stegosaurus* looks awesome in the sand, so does *Tyrannosaurus rex*, or the long, smooth tail of *Brontosaurus*. Use twigs and driftwood to complete the landscape.

SAND MONSTERS

Frighten away the tourists with Everglades creatures. Snakes, alligators, crabs and a crouching panther will make a swampy scene. Add a tangle of sticks and twigs with some greenery to create a mangrove habitat.

SCHOOLS OF BEACH FISH

Go fishing without the rod and reel. Fish appear to swim through the sand, with pebble scales that catch the sun. Make an entire school.

FEEDING THE GULLS

You can befriend the local gull flock with your stale bread and leftover toast. Collect a plate of scrap bread after each meal. At the end of each day, go down to the water's edge and call, "Here gully, gully, gully." Wait for the first gull to fly by and toss it a small morsel. Within seconds you'll have every gull around sweeping over your head. Try to throw the bread high enough so the gulls will catch it in the air.

Begin every feeding session with the call, "Here gully, gully, gully." You'll be surprised how quickly the gulls learn to recognize your voice and associate it with dinner time!

BEACH MAGIC

Here are some tricks you can do by the water to amaze yourself and your friends.

WATER STANDING UPSIDE-DOWN

If you turn a pail of water upside-down, the water will pour out, right? Fill a small beach pail about half full of water. Swing it back and forth in front of you to build up speed. Then, with your arm straight, swing it in fast circles from your knees right up and over your head. Even when the pail is upside-down at the top, the water will stay in it. Why? As long as the water in the upside-down pail is moving in a circular line very fast, it's easier for the water to stay on track than to dribble off course. The water is held in the pail by centrifugal force. If you stop swinging it and hold it still over your head, watch out!

UPHILL CLIMBING WATER

Water flows downhill but never uphill, right? Dip one end of a dry beach towel in the water and stretch the other end of the towel up and over a rock or shrub out of the water. Come back in an hour and see how far water has crept uphill. Water is made up of tiny particles that tend to hold onto each other and inch up tubes of air. In that way, the water seeps slowly up the empty air spaces in the towel.

TYING WATER IN KNOTS

Try this trick to see how you can bend water and tie it together with your fingers.

With a nail, prick five even holes in a line near the bottom of a plastic container (such as an ice-cream pail). The holes should be about 0.5 cm (¼ inch) apart. Fill the pail with water and set it on a flat spot. Five spouts of water should be coming out. Gently pinch the five spouts together with your finger and thumb. Release quickly so your fingers don't brush against the knot you've made in the water. Why does the water knot? The surface of water forms a strong and elastic-like skin where it meets the air. This is called surface tension. In this trick, you shape the skin slightly.

Some water insects have hairy feet that act like snowshoes, spreading their weight out over the surface of the water so they can walk on the skin — or, in fact, the water.

DEAD CALM

Moving water pushes harder than still water, or does it?

Line up two toy boats so they float beside each other. Fill a plastic spray bottle with water — an empty dish-soap squirt bottle will do. Now spray hard between the two boats. Instead of pushing them apart, the spraying water seems to drive the boats together. The still water on the outside of the boats has greater pressure than the moving water between them. So the greater power of the calm water pushes the boats together and causes the crash.

SAND CRAFTS

S A N D C A N D L E S

These candles are made right on the beach. The sand sticks to the outside of the wax, giving the candle an interesting scratchy surface. They're perfect for the cottage dining table or as summer birthday gifts.

You'll need:
a small garden or beach shovel
string 25 cm (10 inches) long
a short stick
a small ball of Plasticine or other modelling material
old crayons or candle stubs
a clean, empty coffee or apple-juice can
an old double boiler or heavy pot
water
a stove
pot holders

1.
Dig a hole in the sand about 10 cm (4 inches) wide and 20 cm (8 inches) deep.

2.
Tie one end of the string to the middle of the stick. Attach the Plasticine ball to the other end of the string.

3.
Ask an adult to help you melt the crayons or candles. Half fill the large can with candle and crayon stubs. Place the can in the pot.

4.
Half fill the pot with warm water.

5.
Place the pot on a back element of the stove. Turn on to low. The wax will take about 20 minutes to melt. As the wax melts, add more crayons and candles. The melted wax should never more than half fill the can. If you're making a big candle, it's better to melt the wax in two batches.

6.
Using a pot holder, remove the can from the pot and carry the melted wax in the can down to the beach.

7.
Carefully pour the melted wax into the hole in the sand.

8.

Lower the string into the middle of the wax, with the Plasticine weighing it down and the stick lying across the top of the hole, holding the string straight through the wax.

9.

Allow the wax to cool and harden — at least 8 hours.

10.

Use the shovel to ease any sand away from the top rim of the hardened candle. Slowly lift the candle out of the hole. Brush off excess sand with your hands.

SAND GOOP

Ever wanted to take your sand castle back home? Here's how you can make a permanent sand castle.

You'll need:

500 mL (2 cups) sand

250 mL (1 cup) corn starch

15 mL (1 tbsp) powdered alum (available at the drug store)

175 mL (¾ cup) of water

an old pot

a stove

a wooden spoon

newspaper

sandpaper

paints

paintbrush

white glue

1.

Mix the sand, corn starch, alum and water in the pot.

2.

Ask an adult to help you cook the mixture over low heat, stirring constantly.

3.

Remove from heat when it has thickened like Play-Doh. Allow it to cool before using.

4.

Sand goop can be used like any modelling material. Create sand castles, sculptures, paperweights or doorstops. As the name goop suggests, it is messy, so work outside or spread newspaper on a table indoors.

5.

Place your completed work on newspaper and allow it to dry at room temperature for several days.

6.

Buff it with sandpaper to remove loose sand.

7.

You can paint your sculpture or leave it plain. Acrylic or poster paints work well.

8.

Painted sculptures can be sealed by brushing them with white glue.

9.

Any leftover sand goop can be stored for a few days in a tightly sealed container.

HOT AND THIRSTY

For those hot and sticky days of summer, here are some cool treats to quench your thirst.

LEMON SODA

You'll need:
juice of one lemon or orange
glass of water
5 mL (1 tsp) of sugar
5 mL (1 tsp) baking soda

1.
Mix the freshly squeezed juice with water and sugar in a glass.

2.
Add 2 ice cubes and the baking soda.

3.
Stir in some bubbles and drink up. Ahhhhh, now that's refreshing.

ICE POPS

When the corner store is not around the corner, you can make your own Popsicles.

You'll need:
an ice-cube tray
fruit juice
toothpicks or Popsicle sticks broken in half

1.
Fill the ice-cube tray with your favourite fruit juice.

2.
Stick a toothpick into each cube, with the smooth end of the stick in the juice.

3.
Place the tray in the freezer for 3 or 4 hours.

4.
Let the ice warm up for a minute before removing from the tray. Careful — if you pull too hard on the toothpick, it may come out without the frozen fruit juice.

SLUSHIES

Slushies are messy and sticky and perfect for hot days. They're as close to a fairground snowcone as you can get, without the fair.

You'll need:

a spoon

a small clean tin can

250 mL (1 cup) of your favourite juice

1.
Place the spoon in the can.

2.
Fill the can with juice and place it in the freezer for about 2 hours.

3.
When the juice is almost frozen, stir it with the spoon and return it to the freezer for half an hour.

4.
Eat your slushie with the spoon, right from the can.

Try freezing seedless grapes, raspberries or strawberries. When you're hot, thirsty or hungry, pop them into your mouth for a cool treat.

HOT BUGS

Can you hear the heat? Cicadas, or heat bugs, make a loud noise by rubbing together two plates on their abdomens. In the months of July and August, these insects celebrate the heat when the temperature rises above 25°C (80°F).

19

CARDBOARD BOATS

Canoes are a traditional Canadian way to travel. They can be made out of birchbark, aluminum, fibreglass or wood and range in size from one-seaters to 18-m (60-foot) war canoes.

Here's how you can make a waterproof cardboard canoe. Your straw action figures from page 190 will sit nicely on the seat, but don't expect them to do any paddling.

You'll need:

a piece of stiff cardboard 15 cm x 30 cm (6 inches x 12 inches)

a pencil

scissors

markers

a darning needle

fine, strong string

newspaper

a pot

paraffin wax or old candles to half fill the tin can

a large tin can

a stove

pot holders

tongs

1.
Fold the cardboard in half, lengthwise. Draw a side view of a canoe with the bottom of the canoe along the fold.

2.
Cut out the canoe but don't cut along the fold. Reserve 2 pieces of cardboard for seats.

3.
Use markers to decorate the canoe.

4.
Thread the darning needle with about 45 cm (18 inches) of string. Double the string and knot it. Sew the bow and stern of the canoe as shown, using a blanket stitch. (See page 205 for blanket stitch instructions.)

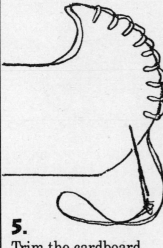

5.
Trim the cardboard seats to fit in the hull of the canoe. Wedge the seats in snugly.

6.
Spread newspaper on your table or kitchen counter, and ask an adult to help with the next step.

7.
Fill the cooking pot with about 5 cm (2 inches) of water. Put the wax in the tin and place it in the pot.

8.
Turn the stove on low until the wax melts. When all the wax is melted, remove the pot from the heat. Using pot holders, take the tin out of the pot and place it on the newspaper.

9.
Holding the cardboard canoe with the tongs, gently dip both ends of the canoe into the wax.

The wax will harden very quickly. You may have to tip the tin to completely cover the canoe. Allow the wax to dry for 10 minutes.

Now you have a waterproofed canoe. You can sail it in shallow water or in the bathtub. Make a fleet of canoes and have a flotilla. You can also make a sail and race your canoe. Just slide two toothpicks between each side of the seat and tape a small square of cloth between them. Catch the breeze and it's smooth sailing!

NATURE DESIGNS

Some Native people artistically decorate clothing and other everyday articles. They get many ideas from nature such as buffalo, owls, deer and snakes, raindrops, mountains or flowers. For some Native people, symbols have special meanings: a rattlesnake jaw stands for strength, butterflies for everlasting life and bear tracks mean something good will happen. Look around outside your cottage. Do you have cliffs, clouds, birds or sunshine that you could draw on the side of your cardboard canoe?

BALLOON- POWERED BOAT

Here's another simple boat to make. This one is propelled with a hot-air balloon. You provide the hot air.

You'll need:
- scissors
- one milk carton
- a bending straw
- heavy-duty tape
- a long balloon
- a nail

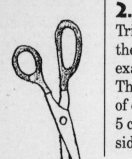

1.
Trim one side off the carton to form the top of the boat. The pouring spout of the milk carton forms the bow.

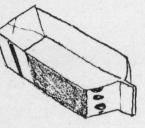

2.
Trim the straw so that the bending part is exactly in the middle. The straight pieces are of equal length - about 5 cm (2 inches) on each side of the bend.

3.
Tape the balloon onto one end of the straw. Pinch the tape on tightly but don't collapse the straw.

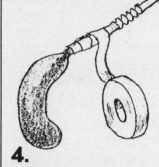

4.
Poke a hole in the bottom of the carton (the stern end).

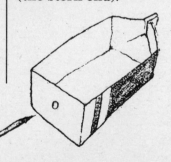

5.
Insert the balloon-straw "propeller" through the hole in the stern. Pull the bending part of the straw through and bend the straw at a 90° angle.

6.
Blow the balloon up. Then hold the end of the straw with one finger.

7.
Now launch your hot-air balloon boat in the lake or your bath.
    You and a friend can race these balloon boats. See who runs out of hot air first.

BALSAM RACERS

Balsam fir is an evergreen tree that grows near lake shores. It has small needles that are green on top and whitish underneath, arranged on twigs in flat sprays. The bark is smooth with bubble-like blisters on it. In pioneer days, people actually made chewing gum using balsam resin as an ingredient. If you have balsam fir trees near your cottage, you can make a few balsam racers.

1.
Using a small stick, poke one end into a blister on the balsam trunk. When you poke a blister with a stick, a gum called resin oozes out. All you need is a small blob of resin.

2.
Lay the stick on the surface of the water with the resin-coated end nearest the shore. The stick will shoot forward, leaving a natural slick in its wake. The racer moves like this because the oil in the resin changes the surface tension of the water. (For more information on surface tension, see page 15.)

3.
Try making several balsam racers and launch them together to see which goes the farthest and the fastest before they "run out of gas."

ECOWATCH
LAST CALL FOR THE LOON

Do you ever wake up to the loons' wild laughter echoing around the lake? Over the last 30 years, people have been making life nearly impossible for loons. These beautiful diving birds have had deformed offspring from eating poisoned fish; they have gone hungry because acid rain has killed off their prey; and now their nesting sites are threatened by power boats. If you are lucky enough to have loons living on your lake, help protect their nests. Drive your boats well out from shore. Make signs saying "No Wake, Nesting Birds" to warn other boaters to stay clear. You can help keep the loons' call from disappearing from your lake.

CRAYFISH TRAP

You see a flash of silver dart underwater. Is it a crayfish waving its claws and checking out your toes? Take another step — and the crayfish vanishes backward into the rocks.

Here's how to make a crayfish trap so that you can get a good look.

You'll need:

2 1-L (1-quart) plastic net berry boxes
4 twist ties
a pocket knife
a thin, bending willow branch
a piece of wiener

1.
Hold two berry boxes so the openings touch each other and then bind them together all the way around with the twist ties. You now have a closed trap.

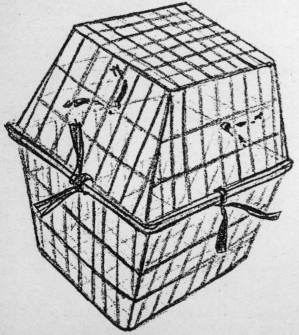

2.
At one end of the trap, slit the plastic net along the bottom edge and part way up two sides to make a flap. Bend the flap into the trap.

3.
Carefully slice the willow branch into 4 6-cm (2 1/2-inch) lengths and sharpen one end of each length. (See Knife Safety on page 117.)

24

4.
Weave 2 of the willow lengths, pointed side first, down the edges of the flap and out through the bottom of the trap. This will hold the flap open and leave a crawl space into the centre of the trap.

5.
Weave 2 more lengths of willow down the middle of the flap but stop before the bottom when the sharp tips point into the trap.

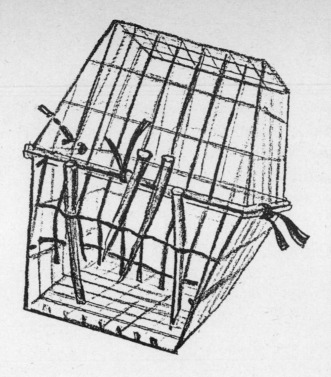

6.
Push a slice of wiener through the crawl space into the trap.

7.
Put the trap underwater near rocks where you've seen crayfish and leave it overnight. You may need to anchor the trap with a stone on a string.

8.
Check your trap in the morning. If you've caught a crayfish, have a good look. To let it go, push the flap in with your fingers and wash the creature out.

SECOND NATURE

Did you know that many people around the world eat crayfish? Crayfish are cousins to shrimp, lobster and crab. Northern varieties are too small for humans to eat but just the right size for a fish like the large-mouthed bass. If a hungry bass snaps at a crayfish but manages to bite off only one claw, the crayfish will simply grow another claw back.

9.
Store the trap out of the water so you don't accidentally catch something in an unattended trap.

SWAMP THINGS

Where can you find an insect that will pierce the skin of a victim three times its size, turn all the victim's insides into a soup and suck them out? In your local swamp — that's where. Water tigers are just one of many fascinating mini-beasts that live in swamp water. Here's how you can take a closer look at some of these strange creatures.

You'll need:

- a medium-sized pail
- a small plastic container (a margarine or yoghurt container)
- a large glass bottle (such as a huge pickle jar)
- a white sheet or counter top

1.
Carry the pail and plastic container to the nearest still-water pond or swamp. Wear rubber boots and take along a friend.

2.
Stand on a firm spot at the edge of the swamp and dip into the water with your plastic container. When you catch a swamp thing — something small like a wiggling bug or plant — pour it into the pail. Don't pour in muddy water.

3.
When your pail is as full as you can carry, it's time to go home.

4.
Pour the swamp water into your jar and set it on a white sheet or counter top away from the direct sun. Do not cover the jar. (If you have leftover swamp water in the pail, return it to the swamp.)

5.
Have a look every day at your jar. Strange new creatures will suddenly appear when tiny eggs in the rich swamp water hatch. Familiar creatures will drastically change or fall prey to hungry predators. Some will lay eggs you cannot see and then the adults will disappear. You are watching the daily dramas of the swamp.

6.
Add a little fresh swamp water every morning so the creatures will always have a healthy food supply.

7.
After you watch the swamp things for a few days, return the creatures and their water to their natural home in the swamp. Lower your pail right into the swamp and pour out the water slowly.

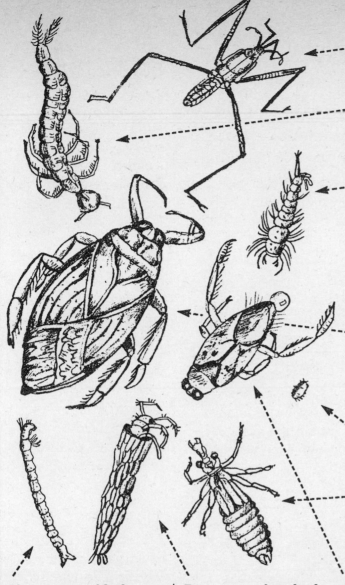

Water striders live on the surface of the swamp and never sink.

The **water tiger** injects into its prey a juice that digests the victim's body before it's eaten.

Mosquito larvae use a breathing tube like a snorkel they stick through the surface of the water. Watch for a mosquito to hatch out of the water, dry its wings and fly away.

The female **giant water bug** cements her eggs onto the back of the male, who then carries them around until they hatch.

That tiny red dot with eight whirling legs is likely a **water mite**.

A **dragonfly nymph** jerks along the bottom because it moves by squirting water out of its behind.

If you see two black eyes on what looks like a see-through body, it's probably a **phantom midge larva**. You can see the phantom midge larvae best if you hold a piece of black paper behind the jar. Like all ghosts, the phantom midge larva is most active at night.

Do you see a bunch of twigs swimming together? It's probably the house of a **caddisfly larva**. Look carefully and a creature will stick its head out one end to grab another piece of construction material. Some varieties will use bits of plant, pebbles or even tiny snails.

A **backswimmer** is a wild scuba diver. That silvery flash at the end of its body is an air bubble, a reserve tank for use until it can get back to the surface. When it's time for a refill, the backswimmer stops paddling and the bubble floats the bug to the surface.

ECOWATCH

It's best not to collect bigger swamp things such as frogs, toads, salamanders or turtles. They don't survive well in a pail or a bottle and are easily injured by people's hands. Don't disturb or collect their eggs either because when they're removed from their natural home, few ever hatch.

Unfortunately, many of our wetlands, such as swamps and marshes, were used as dumps or were drained in past years. Some of the larger swamp creatures became rare. Most people are more careful with wetlands now because they realize wetlands are important storage areas for fresh water as well as breeding grounds for many kinds of wildlife.

If you have a wetland near your cottage, you have a special place. Make sure everybody treats it with care!

FIRST AID

Summer activities bring fun and sometimes cuts, stings, bruises and, of course, sunburn. You can become the cottage medic by preparing a first-aid kit so your family will be prepared.

Keep your first-aid kit in one place — like on top of the refrigerator — so it will be easy to find when you need it. Refill with new supplies if you've had a lot of scraped knees. Then you can enjoy your summer! Don't forget to take your kit with you when you hike or camp out. Put the following supplies in a plastic container with a tight-fitting lid.

strips of sterile cotton to cover major or big cuts

adhesive tape to hold bandage in place

sharp needle to remove slivers or thorns

soap and washcloth to clean wounds

bandages to protect cuts and help stop bleeding

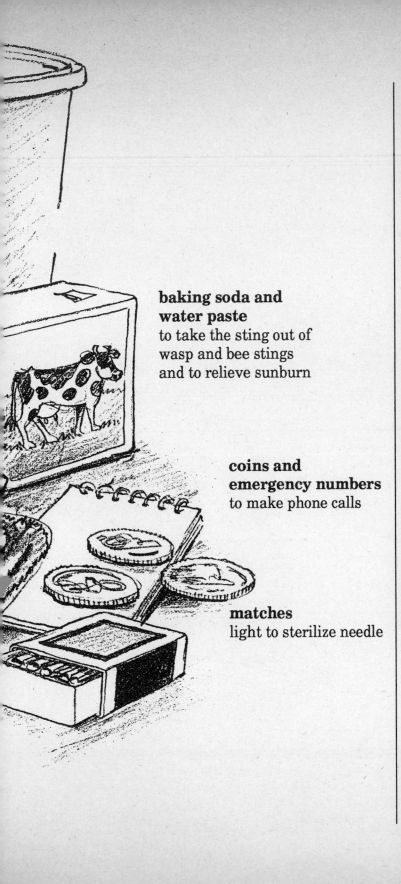

baking soda and water paste
to take the sting out of wasp and bee stings and to relieve sunburn

coins and emergency numbers
to make phone calls

matches
light to sterilize needle

ECOWATCH

Hippos and elephants know enough to cover themselves with mud to protect their skin from the sun's ultraviolet rays. Your skin needs protection, too. Wear a sun hat and loose long-sleeved, long-legged clothing. Hold your clothes up to the light. If you can see right through them, then the sun's rays can travel through them, too. It's best to wear baggy, tightly woven cotton. Also, use a good sun screen and cover up sensitive skin with total block. Zinc oxide ointment acts as a total sun block — just like the mud on the hippo.

WATERFRONT SAFETY

Along with water fun goes water safety. Learn the following water safety rules and make a poster to hang in your cottage or boathouse.

1.
Always swim with a buddy.

2.
Learn where the water is a safe depth for swimming. Walk out and swim in.

3.
Swim parallel to the shore, never straight out into deep water.

4.
Dive only into deep water. Never dive into rocky shallows or unknown waters.

5.
Keep clear of boats and water skiers.

6.
Use inflatable tubes and toys with care. Currents and wind can quickly blow you into deep water.

7.
Keep your beach clean. Never throw glass or cans into the lake.

8.
Keep a reach pole or paddle and life jackets handy for rescues.

SAFETY ALERT

Even if you weigh only 35 kg (75 pounds), you can still rescue an adult. If you see another swimmer struggling close to shore, hold onto one end of the reach pole and, lying flat on the dock or shore, reach out to the swimmer. Speak calmly and encourage the swimmer. Never swim out — a frantic swimmer can pull you under.

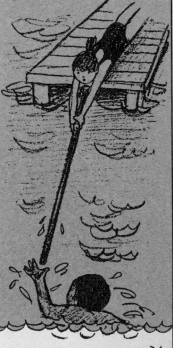

SWIM GAMES

Many land games can be adapted to the water, and waterproof toys can be taken into the lake and used there, too. So get a team together, get wet and have fun.

MARCO POLO

You'll need three or more players for this game.

1.
Decide on the area being used for the game — such as from the boat to the dock, to the sand bar, etc. You'll want an area about the size of a big swimming pool.

2.
One person is It and she must keep her eyes shut.

3.
The It person calls out, "Marco." All other players must reply, "Polo." It keeps calling out "Marco" as often as she wants, swimming in the direction of the nearest Polo. The other players try to swim away without attracting attention. They aren't allowed to dive underwater.

4.
The person who is It is allowed to call out "Submarine" and swim underwater with her eyes open. She must close her eyes when she resurfaces. You are allowed only two "submarines" each time you are It, so save them up for when you really need them!

5.
The person who is It, keeping eyes shut, tries to catch a Polo. As soon as she touches another person, that person becomes It.

COLOURS

This game requires at least three people. It is a category game and can be played with colours or any other category such as cars, baseball teams or birds. The object of the game is to get to the safe zone when the person who is It calls out your colour.

1.
Determine the boundaries of the game as in Marco Polo. The game begins at one end and the safe zone is at the other end.

2.
One person is It. She stands with her back to the water, on the shore, dock or diving board.

3.
The other players stand, or tread water, in a line in the water close to the person who is It.

4.
All the players in the water think of a colour. They can whisper their colour to their neighbour or be on the honour system and keep it secret. Don't let the person who is It hear you.

5.
The person who is It starts by calling out colours. "Red, blue, turquoise..." The other players listen for their colour, and once they hear it, they have to swim quickly to the safe zone.

6.
As soon as It hears someone move in the water, she turns around, jumps in and tries to catch the fleeing player.

7.
If the player is touched before reaching the safe zone, that player becomes It.

UNDERWATER GOLF COURSE

As any golfer will tell you, golf balls sink. They are perfect to dive for. Just remember the safety rules when diving for anything. Never dive into unknown water and watch out for rocks.

You'll need:

9 empty plastic bottles with handles and caps
permanent markers
scissors
nylon clothesline rope
9 heavy rocks
9 golf balls
a pail

1.
Collect 9 plastic bottles with their lids. Peel off the labels so they don't come off in the water. Label each bottle, using permanent marker, one through nine.

2.
Set up your golf course in the water, spacing each "hole" about 5 m (16 feet) apart, using the numbered bottles as markers. At the first hole, measure the depth of the water, using your body as a measuring tape. Cut a piece of rope that'll reach the bottom, giving yourself extra rope for tying knots. Attach the rope to a rock at one end and bottle number one at the other. Drop the rock in the water and you've made your first hole.

3.
Continue to set up your course until you have all the bottle markers floating in the water.

4.
Place a golf ball beside each anchor rock and your course is set.

5.
The object of the golf game is to swim the course as fast as possible, gathering all 9 golf balls. If you can't carry all 9 or stuff them in your bathing suit, you'll have to swim to shore and drop them in a pail. Challenge a friend to see who can do it the fastest. Collect the golf balls after each game so that the waves and current don't steal your golf balls!

WATER BASKETBALL

With your own private basketball facilities, you can play by yourself or take turns with a friend.

You'll need:

hammer

an old tire

a dock

nails

a beachball

1.

Ask an adult to help you hammer your tire to the dock using 2 or 3 large nails. Position the tire so that it will be above your head while you tread water in the lake. Choose the opposite side of the dock to where the boat lands or the family swims.

2.

Inflate a beachball and swim about a metre (several feet) away from the tire "hoop." Tread water or stand and take shots at the hoop.

3.

See how many baskets you can get in a minute. Take shots from various angles. Swim up to the hoop for a slam dunk. You don't have to be tall to score in water basketball.

NATURE BREAK

A sandy shore is home to many creatures. Sea gulls, sandpipers and piping plovers nest on shorelines. They also probe the sand for tasty insects or tiny shellfish. Waders such as yellowlegs scour the shallows for minnows, water worms, snails and crayfish. Grasses and reeds hide frogs and small fish from hunters such as bitterns and great blue herons. River otters dig for clams and muskrats forage for water-lilies, arrowhead and bulrush. Ducks and loons help themselves to insect larvae and minnows close to the shore.

MAKE A SNORKEL

Legs splashing, hands paddling, bathing suits bobbing — people playing in the water must look and sound strange to fish. Get a fish-eye view by making your own snorkel.

You'll need:

a long stalk of horsetail (it's also called scouring rush — see the box on the next page)

a swimming mask

1.
Pick a long stem of horsetail. Pull off the cone and pinch the joints from bottom to top.

2.
Blow and inhale carefully through the stem until you know you've got a clear airway.

3.
Put on your swimming mask and carry your rush snorkel into the water. Find a place to steady yourself and slowly submerge your eyes and ears into the water.

4.
Put the snorkel into your mouth and direct it in a long arch up into the open air. Blow any water out and breathe in, carefully at first, to be sure you aren't sucking water. Now breathe, watch and listen.

HORSETAIL

Horsetail (also called scouring rush and horsepipe) grows in patches on sandy banks and moist slopes. It has a finely grooved, dark green stem with no branches and a small cone at the top. The stem is divided evenly into segments, each one with a skirt of green and black teeth at the joints. In dinosaur times, plants like this grew into trees as tall as a ten-storey building. But since then, horsetails grow to be only about as tall as you.

Plains Indians once used them to make brooms and mats. Ojibwa and European pioneers scrubbed and cleaned their kettles and pans with this plant. For making a snorkel, the important feature of the horsetail is that it's hollow.

UNDERWATER SOUNDS

When you're breathing with your horsetail snorkel underwater, listen. Recognize the sounds? Try shifting rocks on the bottom. You'll notice that sound travels faster underwater and seems to be much louder. Get your ears out of the water if something as noisy as a motor boat starts up!

37

HAND-PADDLING RAFT

On hot sweltering days, you'll want to stay in the water a long time. For a change from swimming, why not make yourself a hand-paddling raft?

You'll need:

an adult helper

a board just longer than three inner tubes lined up

a hand saw

sandpaper

paint and paintbrush (optional)

3 car tire inner tubes (ask at a gas station for used, patched tire inner tubes filled with air)

a pencil

a drill

10 m (32 feet) nylon rope

life jackets

1.
Ask an adult to help you cut the sharp corners off the board with the hand saw and sand all sides of the board, including the edges and the corners.

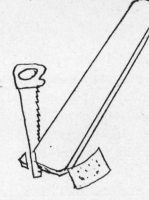

2.
Turn the board face down, line up the inner tubes on the board and mark where the tubes cross the board (4 lines per tube).

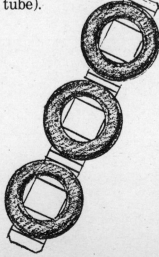

3.
Remove the tubes and ask an adult to help you drill 2 holes side by side along every line you traced (24 holes). Sand around the drill holes.

4.
If you want to paint the board, this is the time to do it. Wait until the paint dries before proceeding.

5.
With the tubes lined along the board, lace the nylon rope through the holes, over the tubes and under the board at each point where the tube meets the board.

6.
Tie off the beginning and end of the rope so the tubes are bound to the board.

7.
Put on your bathing suit and life jacket and head to the beach. Launch the raft board-side up. You can sit with legs dangling into the water over the board or lie along the length of the board face down, tummy wet. Paddle and direct the raft with your hands or a paddle.

THE BIG TUBE

It's always worth a stop by the municipal or township road maintenance shed to ask if they have any used inner tubes from their road graders, monster gravel trucks or earth movers. A local farmer might have an old tractor tire inner tube. These gigantic inner tubes can be patched and filled with air at a gas station. They make terrific, huge floating toys — even in the shallowest water.

DIVING RAFT

Some people think every cottage needs a raft just as much as it needs a sink, a cook stove, a toilet or beds for sleeping. Ask your parents for any construction leftovers — and their time — so you can make a raft.

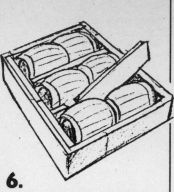

You'll need:
an adult helper
sandpaper
a full sheet of 2-cm (1/2-inch to 3/4-inch) plywood, smooth one side if possible
a drill with large and small drill bits
wood planking about 15 cm wide by 3 cm deep (6 inches by 1 inch) and enough length to run around the outside of the plywood twice (the planking can be in several pieces)
a hand saw
a screwdriver
wood screws about 10 cm (4 inches) long
empty, plugged, small barrels or leftover Styrofoam insulation
marine paint and paintbrush
a heavy, flat rock for an anchor
5 m (16 feet) rope

1.
Sand the plywood well, especially the edges and the corners.

2.
Ask an adult to help you drill a 2-cm (3/4-inch) hole in one end of the wood planking to tie the anchor rope through. Sand carefully around the drill hole and at the ends of each piece of wood planking.

3.
Move all your materials down to the beach. Once assembled, the raft will be too heavy to carry far.

4.
Arrange the wood planks under the plywood so they're lined up flush to the edges all around and they are at a right angle to the plywood.

5.
Starting from the plywood top side, screw wood screws into the wood planks all around. It's easier to screw if you drill a narrow hole through the plywood and just into each plank first to get started.

6.
Turn the raft upside-down again. Cut the remaining planks the right lengths so they form tight frames around the barrels (or pieces of leftover Styrofoam insulation). Screw the frames down, again from the topside of the raft.

7.
Paint the top and sides. Leave it to dry.

8.
Find a big, flat rock and tie the anchor rope to it (see page 47). Run the line through the anchor hole and lay it and the rock in the centre of the raft.

9.
Now is the time to launch your raft and paddle it to where you want it to float for the summer. Remember, the water under your raft should be absolutely free of rocks in all directions and at least 4 m (13 feet) deep if you're planning to dive from it. Even if you don't dive, others who visit the raft may want to.

10.
Hold the free end of the rope and drop anchor. When it hits bottom, tie off the end you're holding, leaving a little slack so the raft is easy to untie and float to shore for winter.

ECOWATCH

Styrofoam pollutes the air and contributes to the greenhouse effect in its manufacture and when it's burned at a dump. Using leftovers in a diving raft is a great way to recycle it rather than sending it to the dump. However, if you don't have any around, don't go out and buy it especially for the raft. Use empty, sealed barrels or large containers that are used to hold roofing tar or cement block sealants instead. Look for containers the same size.

DIVING

Watch a kingfisher, a tern or an otter dive. It's amazing — head first, slip, and they're gone! When you dive, you'll use a different movement. From the standing position, people have to lift their feet up and over. Jump, lift, clear and then head-first and down... Always dive with your arms outstretched in front of you — it looks better and also provides protection against head injury.

CANOE TIPS AND STROKES

Y̶ou can use a canoe as a means of transportation, just like the voyageurs did 200 years ago. That'll mean good, strong strokes and no lily dipping. Or you can put a sweatshirt over the handles of two paddles, stick them between the gunwales, catch the wind and canoe-sail your way down the lake.

To canoe, you'll need to learn how to get in and out of the canoe without getting wet and learn the proper strokes. Choose a calm day without wind or waves for practising. Grab a life jacket and ask an adult or friend to come along.

THE ANATOMY OF A CANOE

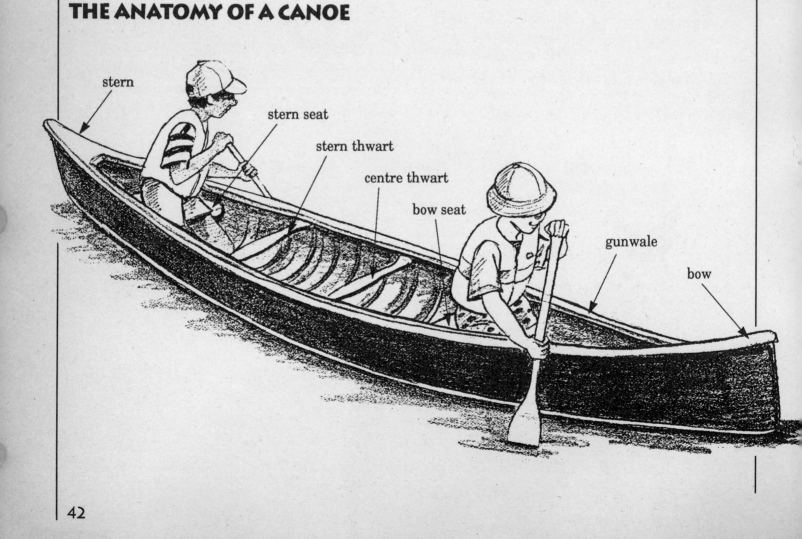

ACCESSORIES

Each person in the canoe needs a paddle that is the right size. Choose a paddle that is no higher than your chin. You'll also need a certified life jacket and an optional kneeling pad or cushion. Don't forget a sun hat or sun screen.

GETTING IN AND OUT

Decide first who will be in the bow and who in the stern. The bowperson must watch for rocks, shallows and other obstacles while paddling. The sternperson does the steering.

If you leap into a canoe the way you get into a power boat, the canoe will tip you out in a flash. Approach a canoe with caution.

The bowperson gets in first while the sternperson holds the gunwale to steady the canoe. Grip your paddle with two hands and hold it across your waist.

Get into the canoe in the middle section of the boat, stepping into the flat centre of the bottom.

Place the paddle across the gunwales and bend your knees for balance.

Now proceed to the bow, crawling over the thwarts slowly, using the paddle across the gunwales to steady yourself.

The sternperson gets in last, while the bowperson steadies the canoe either with the paddle on the bottom of the lake or by holding onto the dock or shore.

Get out of a canoe in the opposite way — the sternperson gets out first and the bowperson follows carefully.

43

CANOE STROKES

There are four parts to any stroke: the catch, pull, recovery and feather.

THE STRAIGHT STROKE

Grip the handle of the paddle in one hand at shoulder level and grasp the shaft just above the blade at gunwale level. Bring the upper hand (gripping the handle) across your chest towards your opposite hip. This will catch the water with the blade of the paddle.

Pull through to your hip.

THE J-STROKE

The J-stroke is a steering stroke. It is exactly like the straight stroke in the catch and pull stages, but then the sternperson steers by following a "J" path to the end of each straight stroke. The recovery and feather are the same as the straight stroke.

To recover the blade, swing it towards the bow. Feather it, to cut down on wind resistance, by turning it flat so that the blade is parallel to the water.

Repeat this in a steady rhythm. Try to use all the muscles in your upper body when you're paddling. If you use just your arm muscles, your arms will get tired quickly.

45

KEEP YOUR BOAT AFLOAT

Here's how to keep your boat shipshape. With a trim boat and a knowledge of boat safety, your summer will be smooth sailing.

WITHOUT KEYS, YOU'RE SUNK

If your power boat has a key, or your cottage is on an island, a key float is a great thing to make.

You'll need:

a corkscrew

a cork

twist ties

a key

1.
Using a corkscrew, enlarge the hole in the middle of a cork by twisting the corkscrew in at both ends. Check that you have a hole all the way through the cork by holding it up to the light to see through it.

2.
Insert one large twist tie or two small twist ties, twisted together, through the hole in the cork.

3.
Thread the key onto one end and twist the ties together.

4.
Test for buoyancy in a full sink of water. If it sinks, try a larger cork or add another.

ANCHOR ROCK

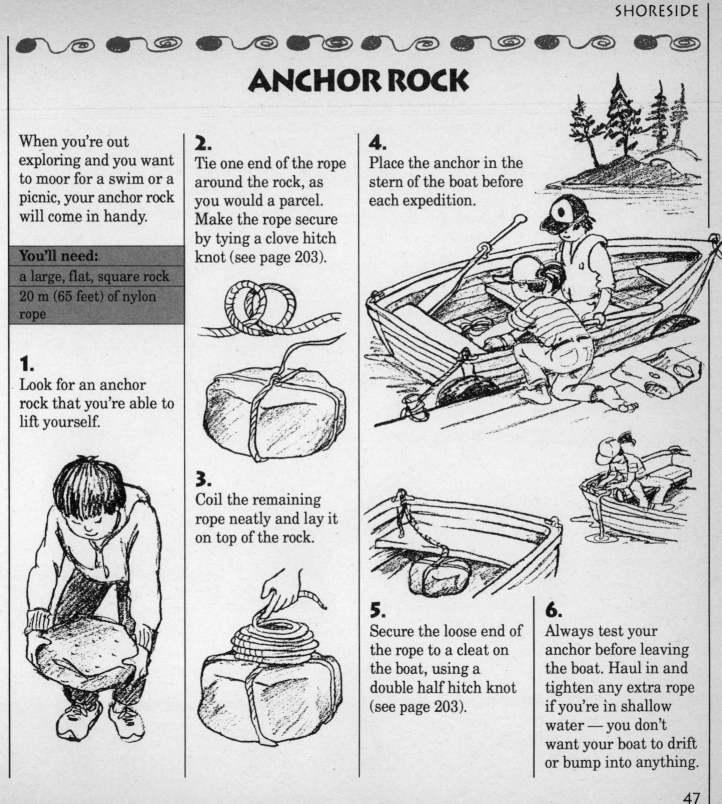

When you're out exploring and you want to moor for a swim or a picnic, your anchor rock will come in handy.

You'll need:

a large, flat, square rock

20 m (65 feet) of nylon rope

1.
Look for an anchor rock that you're able to lift yourself.

2.
Tie one end of the rope around the rock, as you would a parcel. Make the rope secure by tying a clove hitch knot (see page 203).

3.
Coil the remaining rope neatly and lay it on top of the rock.

4.
Place the anchor in the stern of the boat before each expedition.

5.
Secure the loose end of the rope to a cleat on the boat, using a double half hitch knot (see page 203).

6.
Always test your anchor before leaving the boat. Haul in and tighten any extra rope if you're in shallow water — you don't want your boat to drift or bump into anything.

SAILOR'S BAILER

If it rains or you are sprayed with waves, a bailer will help keep the boat from swamping (when a boat fills with water and sinks). Modify a plastic jug to make a non-rusting bailer.

You'll need:

a pen

a large plastic jug with a handle

a sharp knife or scissors

1.
Using the pen, draw a line half-way around the jug about 5 cm (2 inches) from the bottom, up the middle, along the ridge below the handle and back down to the line around the bottom.

2.
Hold the jug by the handle and carefully cut along the line.

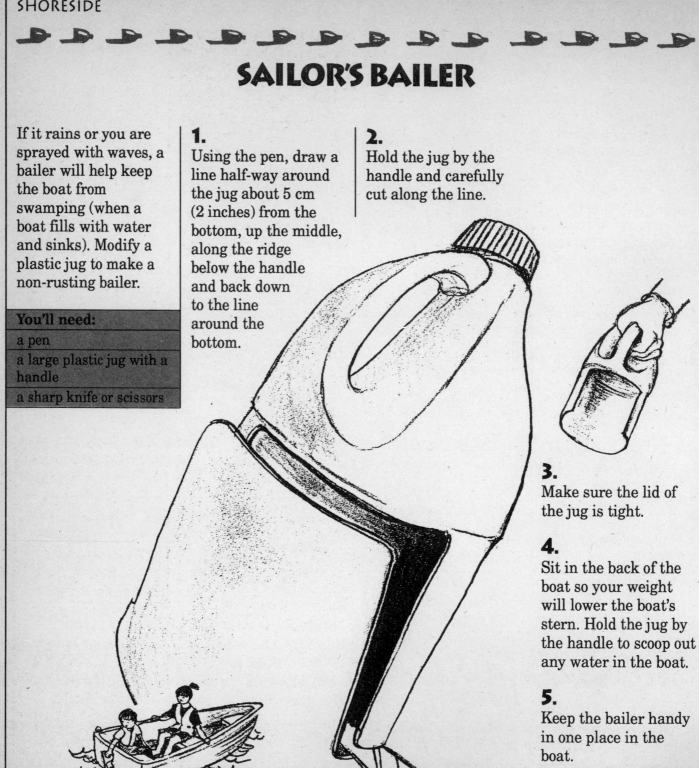

3.
Make sure the lid of the jug is tight.

4.
Sit in the back of the boat so your weight will lower the boat's stern. Hold the jug by the handle to scoop out any water in the boat.

5.
Keep the bailer handy in one place in the boat.

BOAT
RULE BOX

Some things are the law, some things are common sense. The following should always be in your boat:

1.
One government-approved life jacket or floating cushion for each person in the boat.

2.
One sailor's bailer.

3.
Two oars or paddles in case of engine failure.

4.
One emergency kit in a waterproof container. (See page 28.)

5.
Keep a flashlight in the emergency kit for signalling for help. See the box on this page to learn the Morse code signal.

6.
Turn to page 42 for canoe tips.

SIGNAL FOR HELP

Watch the water for the twinkling lights of boats. Would you be able to tell if a boat was in distress and signalling for help? Engine failure in a power boat or lack of wind for sailboats are common crises on cottage lakes. If you see a light flashing in a repeated pattern — pay attention. The international Morse code signal for HELP! is three short blinks, three long blinks, then three short blinks, followed by a pause and then the signal is repeated.

. . . — — — . . .

If someone is calling out for help, get an adult and go to the rescue if it is practical or telephone the police for help. Larger lakes have police launches or the local constabulary will ask local boaters for help.

ECOWATCH

You can help keep your lake alive and clean by thinking about everything you add to the lake. If you must use a motor boat, keep joy-riding to a minimum and have a destination in mind. If you have oars, use them — it's better for you and the lake. Canoeing, sailing and windsurfing don't pollute, and you can get a closer look at the shoreline and what lives there. Don't throw any junk or garbage into the lake. Make sure your family cleans with phosphate-free detergents or pure soap, and never dumps soapy water directly into the lake.

MAKE A WATERSCOPE

On the edges of most lakes, you can find shallow reedy marshes that are great for exploring. Make a waterscope to get a close-up look at the creatures living there. Paddle your boat over to the reeds and peer in.

You'll need:
a knife
a large plastic container such as an ice-cream or yoghurt container
some clear plastic wrap
a strong elastic band

1.
Ask an adult to help you cut the bottom out of the plastic container.

2.
Stretch clear plastic wrap over the bottom and secure it with a strong elastic band.

3.
Lower the plastic-covered end into the water. It should be watertight enough that you can hold it several centimetres (a few inches) into the water and get a clear view of what's down there.

Point your waterscope to look under a water-lily. Look for bass hiding in the leafy shadow and along the stem to the muddy bottom.

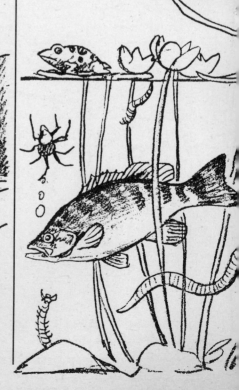

Flowering plants such as arrowhead and pickerelweed keep their roots wet close to shore. Look for frogs, water snakes and leeches hunting among their stems and roots.

Tall, slender plants such as reeds and bulrushes sway with wind and waves without breaking or tearing. The straight, underwater stems make a forest of hiding places for minnows and dragonfly larvae. Look on the stems for the see-through cases the larvae leave behind when they fly off as adult dragonflies.

Great blue herons and American bitterns stand still in the shallow water, ready to strike. Their long legs look like reeds from underwater, and minnows or frogs who can't tell the difference get speared for lunch.

Right near the shore where it's almost too overgrown and shallow for your boat, your waterscope lens will pick out all sorts of tiny creatures in the water. Turn to Swamp Things on page 26 to find out more about them.

LANDSIDE

Turn inland and there's tons to do. Fly a kite or construct a flagpole, build a fort or a bluebird house, track time or maybe snakes, net bugs or investigate an anthill. If you can't decide, make a hammock and lie down with a good book and a refreshing drink. It's up to you.

SWING INTO SUMMER

No cottage is complete without a swing or two. On hot days, they create wind to blow through your hair. When you're mad or sad, you can shout or sing as you swing.

STEEL-BELTED FUN

You'll need:

an adult helper
a tire or inner tube
3 m (10 feet) of strong rope
a ladder
a sturdy tree limb

1.
Look around in the shed for an old tire, or take a trip to the dump. Choose a tire that isn't ripped, studded or chained. If you want a soft swing, ask the mechanic at the local garage for an old inner tube. You can have it inflated at the garage or use it floppy.

2.
Ask an adult to help you site your swing. The tree has to be located away from buildings, hydro wires and roads.

3.
Tie a loop knot around the tire (see page 203). Using a ladder, and with help from an adult, tie the rope to a strong right-angled branch using a double half hitch (see page 203). Climb back down again.

4.
Tie the tire so that it swings about a metre (3 feet) off the ground. Get swinging!

BOARD SWING

You'll need:

a piece of board 30 cm x 50 cm (12 inches x 20 inches)
a saw
a drill
sandpaper
rope
a ladder

1.
Ask an adult to help you cut the board to the required measurements using a hand saw.

2.
Choose a drill bit a little bigger around than your rope. Ask your adult helper to drill a hole in the middle of each end of the board about 10 cm (4 inches) in from the end.

TARZAN ROPE

3.
Using medium sandpaper, hand sand the board so you won't get any slivers. Make sure you sand well along the edges.

4.
Thread the rope through the top of one hole, run the rope along the bottom of the swing and thread the rope through the bottom of the other hole. Pull the rope through until you have equal lengths of rope at each end.

5.
Site your swing, as in the tire swing, allowing about 50 to 75 cm (20 to 30 inches) clearance for your legs. Tie both ropes on the tree branch, using double half hitches (see page 203). Now, get in the swing!

You'll need:
2.5 m (8 feet) of rope at least 2 cm (3/4 inch) thick
a tree to swing from
a ladder

1.
Tie knots in your rope at 40-cm (15-inch) intervals. The knots will help you climb up.

2.
Site your tree as you did for the tire swing.

3.
Tie the rope to the branch of your swing tree using a loop knot (see page 203).

4.
Wrap your legs around one of the knots, hold on tight and kick off from the tree. Let out a Tarzan "AHAHAHA HAHAHAH!"

55

VEGETABLE GARDEN

Do you like to have a say in the menu? Why not start a vegetable garden and grow what you like to eat! This is a great project, especially if you spend most of the summer at the cottage.

You'll need:
a round-mouth shovel
peat moss and/or compost
vegetable seeds
string
sticks for stakes
a hoe or garden rake
a hose and water

1.
Choose a sunny spot, within reach of the hose, for your garden. Stake out the boundaries — 2 m (7 feet) by 3 m (10 feet) will be enough for starters. Check your spot with an adult to make sure it's okay to dig there.

2.
Remove the grass with the round-mouth shovel. Use the sod to patch bare spots on the rest of your lawn.

3.
Prepare the soil by turning over the entire area, chopping up and loosening the soil with each shovelful. Dig in peat moss and/or compost to break up and enrich the soil.

4.
Choose vegetable seeds that germinate quickly and have a short growing season. Look on the back of the seed packets for the information on each variety. Peas, lettuce, beans, spinach and Swiss chard are all good. Buy chives and marigold seeds for pest control. Avoid carrots, beets, pumpkin and zucchini. They all require a long growing season. (If you go to your cottage in May or early June, you can start these varieties then.)

5.
Using the string and two stakes, mark out each garden row. Using a hoe or the corner of a rake, dig a trough for each variety of seeds. Leave at least 30 cm (12 inches) between rows. You'll need the space for walking and weeding, and the plants need space to grow.

6.
Read the directions on each pack of seeds. The depth for planting varies from vegetable to vegetable. Cover the seeds with soil and tap lightly. Plant the chives and marigold seeds around the edges of the garden. Insects and small animals don't like the smell of these plants and are less likely to help themselves to the lettuce.

7.
Water the entire garden well after planting. Soak the soil with a gentle sprinkle, otherwise you will dislodge the seeds.

8.
Water your garden regularly and generously. The summer heat can dry out and kill the seedlings and plants. It's best to water in the early morning or in the evening when the sun is low in the sky and less water will evaporate.

9.
While you're waiting for the plants to peek above the soil, make some of the wildlife-friendly deterrents on the next two pages.

MAKE A **SCARECROW**

You'll likely share some of your garden food with rabbits and raccoons, but a scarecrow and several pinwheels should help you keep most of your crop.

You'll need:

a hammer and nails

1 2-m (7-foot) long piece of wood 5 cm x 10 cm (2 inches x 4 inches — most people will know what you mean if you ask for a two-by-four)

1 board for the arms

a plastic bag

newspaper

string

a permanent marker

1 large old shirt

wild grasses, a sun hat or other things to decorate your scarecrow

1.
Nail the two pieces of wood into a "t" shape.

2.
Hammer the "t" into the soil of the garden.

3.
Fill the plastic bag with scrunched-up newspaper. Gather it at the neck and tie it together with a piece of string.

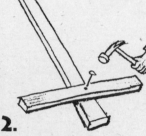

4.
Draw a fierce face on the plastic bag face.

5.
Fasten the face to the top of the "t" with string around the neck.

6.
Using the crossbar of the "t" as arms, dress the scarecrow with a shirt. The flapping shirt-tails will frighten away some animals.

7.
Jazz up the scarecrow with a sun hat, a fly swatter or a hoe attached to the sleeve and use wild grasses for hair.

PEST-CONTROL PINWHEELS

You'll need:

a thin piece of plastic 15 cm x 15 cm (6 inches x 6 inches) (plastic windows from cartons will do)

a ballpoint pen

a ruler

scissors

a thumb tack with a long needle

a chopstick or thin, straight stick

1.
Mark the centre of the plastic square with the ballpoint pen. Label the four corners 1, 2, 3 and 4, starting with the top left corner.

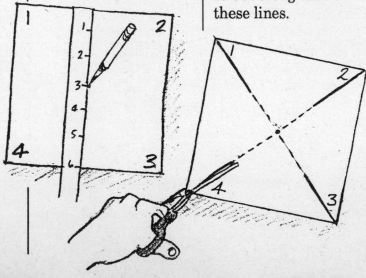

2.
Draw a faint "X" through the midpoint of the square, joining 1 and 3 with one line and 2 and 4 with another.

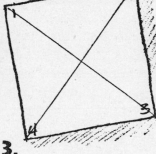

3.
Measure and mark the point that is half-way between the midpoint and each of 1, 2, 3 and 4. Cut along each of these lines.

4.
Fold the lower half of corner 1 to the mid-point, followed by the upper half of corner 2, the upper half of corner 3 and the lower half of corner 4.

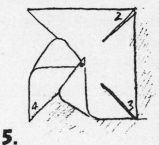

5.
Push a thumb tack through all four corner pieces at the midpoint of the square and into the stick.

Make several pinwheels and place them around the garden, in the ground, on a fence or attached to the scarecrow.

ECOWATCH

You can make sure your garden is chemical-free. If you get an infestation of bugs, don't rush off to buy spray. Many pests can be chased away using non-toxic (non-poisonous) methods. Collect ladybugs (ladybirds) and put them into the garden because they love to feast on some pesky bugs. Or make a solution of 15 mL (1 tablespoon) of mild soap (such as Ivory Liquid) mixed with 250 mL (1 cup) of water. Sprinkle it on bug eggs, larvae or insects.

SUMMER GARBAGE

Up at the cottage, far from city recycling programs, you can't forget to reduce, reuse and recycle. Smart shopping and taking recyclables back to the city will help, but you can make your cottage "greener" by making your own composter.

You'll need to build a solid structure that will hold the waste, heat up, let in air, keep out pesky critters and have an opening for stirring and scooping out the compost. Try to make one without buying any materials. Here are some design ideas.

MINI COMPOSTER

Starting small might get your family composting. Use an old, large, rectangular laundry basket. With a nail and hammer, make drainage holes in the bottom. For a lid, use a piece of plywood bigger than the basket. Put a large, heavy rock on top to keep out raccoons. Place in a sunny spot away from the cottage or picnic area.

IT'S A PIT

Select a site for your composting pit. Check with an adult before you start digging — you don't want to unearth cables or the septic tank. Dig a hole about a square metre (square yard) and as deep as possible — up to 1 m (3 feet). An old screen window makes a good lid. It lets in moisture, lets out smells and keeps out compost thieves.

THE CARPENTER'S COMPOSTER

If you are good with a hammer and nails and have an adult who can help you, try making this wooden composter. Using two-by-fours, make a frame that is 1 m (3 feet) square and 1 m (3 feet) tall. The sides can be covered with lattice, plywood with holes drilled in it or with chicken wire. A heavy square of plywood makes a good lid. Don't forget the rock "lock."

COMPOST CUISINE

Perfect compost is like a layered salad. You need ingredients from your beach, your lawn, your kitchen and your garden. Start with a layer of beach stones on the bottom of your composter or in your pit. Next comes a layer of grass cuttings, leaves or trimmings from a hedge or bush. Then a kitchen waste layer. You can compost all vegetable matter, coffee grounds, tea bags, eggshells and unbleached paper. (Don't put in meat, dressings, cereal or dairy products — they smell and attract flies and larger creatures.) Top this with a shovelful of soil. Sprinkle with water. Stir occasionally. Continue to feed your composter all summer long.

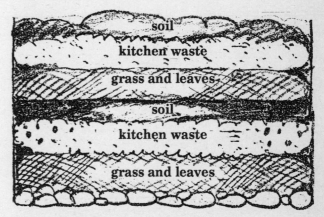

Your compost will have to "cook" for about a year. It's like a good stew — it needs to simmer and mix its flavours for a long time. But don't worry, your garden will be hungry for compost goodness next spring. Shovel the compost, which looks like rich, black soil, onto the flower or vegetable garden. Dig it in before planting time. Compost can also be used to enrich hanging baskets or planters.

MORE

MAKE YOUR OWN HAMMOCK

There is nothing like a hammock on a lazy, hazy summer day. You can hang out, swing or stare at the clouds while lolling in the folds of a hammock. They are simple to make. The tough part will be getting your parent out of the hammock so you can have a turn.

You'll need:

- a sturdy cotton sheet, single-bed size
- straight pins
- polyester thread
- a sewing needle
- a measuring tape
- 1 dime (coin)
- a pencil
- heavy-duty thread
- a large sewing needle
- a thimble (optional)
- scissors
- 2 trees about 2.5 m (8 feet) apart
- 1 50-m (165-foot) clothesline rope
- 2 large tethering rings (available at hardware stores)
- 2 sturdy screw hooks

1.

Fold the ends of the sheet over at the hem to form a double thickness. Pin this with straight pins.

2.

Using the polyester thread and the regular sewing needle, sew the folded ends with a blanket stitch (see page 205).

3.

At each end, measure the width of your sheet and find the centre. Using the dime and pencil, mark a circle on the hem. Measure and mark circles at 20-cm (8-inch) intervals to both edges. These circles mark where you will make grummets, or reinforced holes, for threading the rope through.

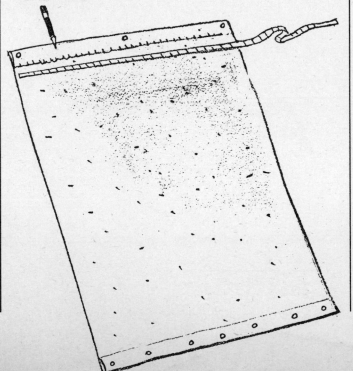

4.

Using 1 m (3 feet) of heavy-duty thread, thread the large needle, pull the threads double and knot them together (see page 205).

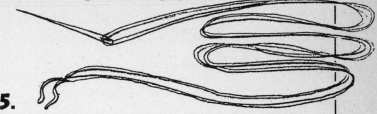

5.

To make the grummets, begin by pulling the needle from the wrong side of the sheet into a pencil-marked circle on the right side of the sheet. Sew stitches 1.5 cm (³/₄ inch) in length all the way around the outside of the circle. Don't worry if the stitches overlap, that will only make your grummet stronger. Tie off the thread when you have completed the circle.

MORE

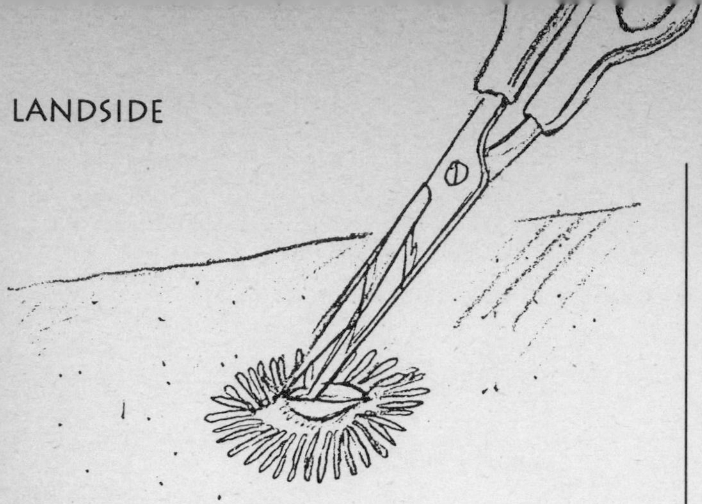

8.

Cut one piece of rope for each grummet you have sewn. If you have 16 grummets, cut 16 pieces of rope 2 ½ times the distance between the end of the hammock and the tree.

6.

Using the sharp point of the scissors, open the centre of the circle, taking care not to cut the stitching. Repeat this procedure for all the circles.

7.

Lay the hammock on the ground between the two trees. Measure the distance from the ends of the hammock to the trees.

9.
Thread each rope through the grummets and lay them double. Gather all the rope pieces and tie them to the tethering ring using a square knot (see page 204).

10.
Screw the hooks into the trees about 1.5 m (5 feet) off the ground. You may want to ask an adult to help you.

11.
Loop the tethering ring over the hook. Now quickly hop into the hammock before anyone else does.

12.
Take the hammock indoors if you expect rain and when you pack up the cottage at the end of the summer.

TELLING TIMES

Long before people had watches or digital clocks, our bodies told us the time of day when our stomachs growled or our eyelids wouldn't stay open. We still don't need a watch to tell us it's mealtime or bedtime — our bodies let us know. It's all the in-between times we need watches for. Make a sundial so you can tell the time without a watch.

You'll need:

a sharp pencil

a piece of string 15 cm (6 inches) long

a piece of wood or thick cardboard about 30 cm (12 inches) long and about 15 cm (6 inches) wide

a squared piece of thin cardboard, such as the side of a cereal box

a ruler

scissors

white glue

2.

Next, make the "hand" of the sundial, called the gnomon. Pick up the piece of thin card by one corner and mark 15 cm (6 inches) along the bottom and 15 cm (6 inches) up the side. Cut diagonally between your two marks to make a triangle.

15 cm (6 inches)

15 cm (6 inches)

1.

Start by making the base of the sundial. Tie the pencil to one end of the string. Hold the free end of the string under your thumb half-way down the edge of the piece of wood. Pull the string tight and draw a semi-circle on the wood from the top to the bottom around your thumb. Now, draw a straight line from where you held your thumb to the opposite edge of the wood.

3.

Using one of the shorter sides, draw a straight line about 1 cm (½ inch) up from the edge and fold along that line to make a flap. You should now have a triangular card with a flap on the bottom.

4.

Glue the flap onto your base as shown.

5.

Place your sundial on a flat spot outside where it'll get full sun all day. Line it up so the gnomon points north. (You can do this at night with the North Star. The North Star is easy to find because it's the one that is "pouring" out of the Big Dipper.)

6.

Now, make the dial of your sundial. Using a watch, mark where the shadow from the gnomon falls on the base every hour and label each mark with its time. Do this all day until you've marked all the hours from sun-up to sundown. From now on, you'll be able to leave your watch inside on sunny days and read the time from your sundial.

NATURAL WATCHES

Just as you have an inner clock to tell when it's lunchtime or bedtime, so do some plants. Learn to read some of these natural clocks.

Marigold flowers, for instance, open each morning by 7 o'clock. Blue chicory and pickerelweed close up at noon. The white water-lily shuts tight every afternoon at 4 o'clock and the marigold closes by 7 p.m. Look around and you'll be able to find other examples of plant clocks to help you tell the time.

CHICORY

PICKERELWEED

Some plants open up on schedule every day even if it's not sunny. When you find a plant clock, cover it with a pail and peek in to see if it still opens and closes on time, even though it's in the dark.

Look for animal clocks, too. Deer flies may bug you after 9 a.m., horseflies at 2 p.m. and pesky mosquitoes by 8 p.m. You can even teach animals to tell you the time. If you put honey on a spoon in the same place at the same time every day, bees will get to expect it and come buzzing — and they won't be late.

FLAGPOLE

Once your cottage has a flagpole, raising and flying a flag will become a tradition. You can make your own personal flag, incorporating classic symbols such as lions and crowns, or imaginative designs that reflect a family hobby or trait. Some families use their flagpole as a signal to friends. When the red flag is waving, stay away, we're napping. When the green flag is up, come on over, we want company. So get some helpers together and hoist that flagpole.

You'll need:

an adult helper

an axe

a 7- to 10-m
(23- to 32-foot) cedar tree

a pruning saw

2 sheets of coarse
sandpaper

a sharp knife

a 3- or 4-cm
(1- or 1½-inch) pulley

20 m (65 feet) of 2-cm
(½-inch) nylon rope

a shovel

a pail of gravel

1 cleat

a flag

1.
With help from an adult, select and cut down a tall, slim, straight tree with a base diameter of about 15 cm (6 inches). Cedar will last longest but poplar or beech will work, too.

2.

Using a pruning saw, trim all the branches close to the trunk.

3.

After pruning, use coarse sandpaper to buff off the roughness.

4.

Skinning the bark off is optional. If you do choose to skin the tree, go slowly. You must use a very sharp knife, always stroking away from yourself. Hold the knife at a 45° angle, cutting to remove the bark without gouging the wood. Cedar bark will peel off in strips once you've started it with the knife (see Knife Safety on page 117).

5.

Attach the pulley about 50 cm (20 inches) from the top of the pole. Do this before you hoist the pole.

6.

Thread the rope through the pulley. Tie a loose knot to keep it from coming out while you raise the pole.

7.

Choose a site for your flagpole that is out in the open and away from hydro lines. Why not down near the water or out on the point?

8.
Using a shovel and lots of muscle, dig a hole about 1 m (3 feet) deep and 75 cm (30 inches) wide. The width of the hole will depend on the size of the butt of the tree you are using.

9.
To raise the flagpole, have one person hold the butt steady over the hole. The other person picks up the pole near the pulley and walks towards the hole, raising the pole hand over hand. (You push the pole ahead of yourself, using your chest and shoulders to support the weight of the pole.) Meanwhile, the first person steers the butt of the pole so it slips easily into the hole.

10.
Then one of you holds the pole straight in place while the other pours a pail of gravel into the hole, then shovels back the soil. Both of you use your feet to tap down the soil firmly.

11.
At chest level, screw the cleat onto the pole.

12.
Because flags must be secured at the top and bottom, the tops of flags usually have a toggle and the bottoms have a small rope coming out of a grummet (a reinforced ring). Stand at the flagpole and figure out which end of your flag is up.

13.
Untie the nylon rope on the flagpole and attach the flag to the toggle using a clove hitch (see page 203).

14.
Let the flag hang down and secure the other end of the rope in the grummet rope, using a sheet bend (see page 204).

15.
Raise the flag to the top of the pole and secure the rope around the cleat.

16.
Your flag will last longer if you take it down during bad weather. Make sure you store it in a dry place during the winter.

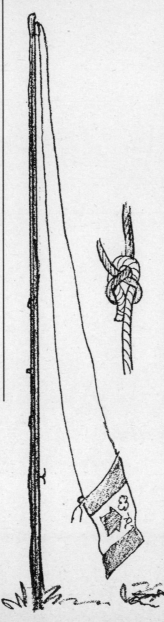

FLAG-FLYING RULES

1.
When flying the national flag, it is considered unlucky or unpatriotic to let the flag drag on the ground.

2.
Traditionally, the national flag is raised after sunrise and lowered before sunset.

3.
When a flag is flying upside-down, it signals "Help."

HELP!

WILDLIFE BLIND

Seeing a wild animal up close in its natural habitat can be very exciting. Get a closer, longer look at wild animals by constructing a wildlife blind beside a marsh, on the beach, in a meadow or at the edge of the forest.

You'll need:

cloth 3 m x 1 m (10 feet x 3 feet)
scissors
string
camouflage material, such as sticks and leaves

1.
Select cloth that will blend in with the surroundings, such as an old piece of burlap, a brown bedspread or an old green tablecloth.

2.
Choose a site for the blind where you have observed animals or birds. Bulrushes, shrubs, tall grasses or sand dunes are great natural hiding places.

3.
Make holes in the four corners of the cloth with the scissors.

4.
Cut 4 pieces of string about 50 cm (20 inches) long. Pull a piece of string through each corner opening and knot one end of the string.

5.
Cut 4 or 5 25-cm (10-inch) slits in the cloth. These will be your peep-holes.

6.

Wrap the cloth around one side of the bulrushes, shrubs or tall grasses close to the ground. Use the strings to secure it in place.

7.

Use grasses, sticks and leaves that you find around your site to camouflage your blind, making it blend in with the surroundings.

8.

If your blind is behind a sand dune, you'll need three sturdy sticks to jab into the sand. Make a V with the sticks, securing the ends of the cloth on the outside two sticks.

9.

After several days, your blind will become part of the scenery, and local wildlife will no longer notice it is there.

10.

Snuggle in behind the blind and quietly wait for any passers-by. Use the peep-holes to see if there are any wild creatures in the area.

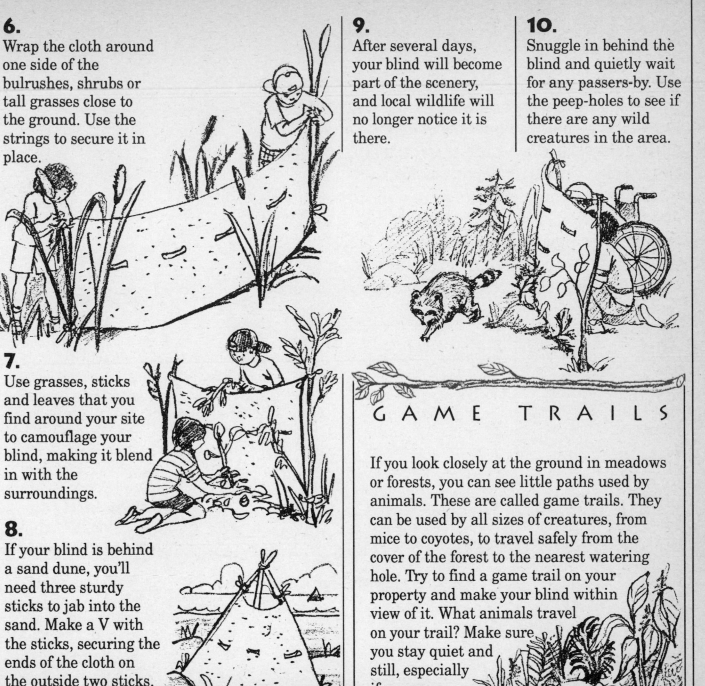

G A M E   T R A I L S

If you look closely at the ground in meadows or forests, you can see little paths used by animals. These are called game trails. They can be used by all sizes of creatures, from mice to coyotes, to travel safely from the cover of the forest to the nearest watering hole. Try to find a game trail on your property and make your blind within view of it. What animals travel on your trail? Make sure you stay quiet and still, especially if you see a skunk.

CALL OF THE WILD

Hunters have always known they can attract wildlife by mimicking their sounds. Northern Native people knew how to call down migrating geese by repeating their honks. Or they could attract moose in dense bush by scraping an antler on spruce bark.

Birds and animals also come to check out squeaky distress calls. They may be friendly and want to help, they may be just curious or they may be predators looking for an easy lunch. On a quiet day, make your own wildlife caller and see who comes to investigate you.

You'll need:

2 Popsicle sticks

a long, wide blade of wild grass (some people use a length of broken cassette tape)

an elastic band

1.
Make sure the Popsicle sticks are clean and dry.

2.
Sandwich a blade of dry grass between the two sticks. Secure one end by wrapping the elastic band around and around it.

3.
Hold the caller up to your mouth, pinch the open end and blow as if playing a harmonica.

4.
To attract wildlife, sit quietly and blow into your caller repeatedly, at the same rhythm and pitch as a crying baby. Waaa Waaa Waaa. See if you attract friend or foe. Blue jays and chickadees may come first. Keep it up and you may spot a fox or hawk.

CRY LIKE A LOON

You can make the mournful cry of a loon with only your hands and mouth.

1.

Hold your hands together loosely as if you were just starting to clap. Keep that position, leaving an air pocket between your palms, but tightening your fingers so the air pocket is surrounded.

2.

Press your two thumbs together so your thumbnails face you. Bend the thumb joints down against your cupped hands. You should see a space below your thumb joints and above the base of your thumbs.

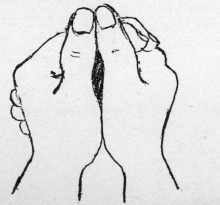

3.

Put the thumb joints to your lips, leaving the hole below the joints free to the air.

4.

Hold your lips loosely, as if you were just getting ready to whistle. Hold back your tongue a little. Blow onto the thumb joints slowly. Adjust the position of your lips until the sound you are producing is full and mournful.

5.

If you hear a loon, return with your own loon call. You may find the loon "talks" back and you can have a conversation. The loon may come closer to see what's up. Then you'll get a good look and see what movements the loon makes to create its call.

SWEEP-NETTING FOR MEADOW BUGS

By the beginning of July, long-grass country is a-buzz with bugs. You'll be amazed at how many different kinds of weird bugs are out there. Here's a net you can make to sweep a meadow and check out the local bugs.

You'll need:

a coil of strong wire or a coat hanger

a tape measure

wire cutters

a penknife

a thin, rigid 3-m (10-foot) stick

masking tape

a roll of thinner wire

an old pillowcase

scissors

a needle

thread

pliers

1.
Snip off 1 m (3 feet) of the strong wire with wire cutters. Bend it to make one large loop. Measure about 15 cm (6 inches) from each end of the loop and bend each end out sharply to form two prongs. (With an adult's help, you could shape a coat hanger to the same shape and size.)

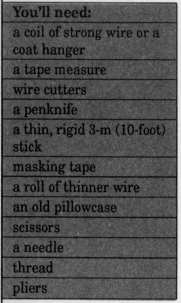

2.
With the penknife, carefully cut two thin ridges into your stick, 15 cm (6 inches) down from the top. Hold the prongs of your wire loop in place just above the ridge and tape them there with masking tape.

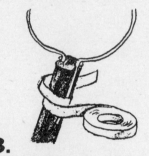

3.
Using the thinner wire, hold one end with your thumb on the stick below the prongs and wind into the ridge you cut. Then keep winding the wire up, tightly around the prongs, until you get to the top of the stick.

4.
Cut the wire leaving a tab of several centimetres (a few inches) of wire sticking out the end. Jab that tab and the one you held down with your thumb back under a couple of the wire coils.

5.
Turn a pillowcase inside-out and spread flat. Place the loop on it about 5 cm (2 inches) from the top opening and touching one double side. Cut a triangular shape from the pillowcase, wide enough at the top to fill the circle of the loop and with the sides tapering to a rounded bottom. You can use the double fold as a side, leaving only one of the sides open, if you cut the mouth at a slight angle.

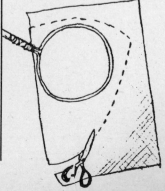

6.

Sew the open side with fine stitches. Turn the case right-side-in so your stitching can't be seen.

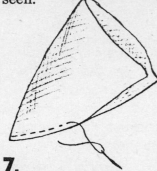

7.

Pull the top of the pillow-case net through your wire loop and fold the cloth back over the rim. Fold the rough edge under again to form a hem and stitch the net into place.

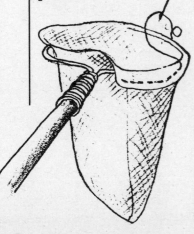

HOW TO SWEEP-NET

Choose a sunny afternoon and head for a meadow with your net and a shoe box. Start anywhere in the meadow. Leaving the box on the ground, hold the net at plant-top level and brush quickly up and down and around the field. When you've circled back to the box, carefully shake your catch into it, turning the net inside-out to release all the clingers. See if you've got any of the insects listed here.

When you've finished looking at your bugs, turn the box on its side and let them hop back into the meadow.

The treehopper is a tiny bug that looks like a thorn.

Katydids are all-green grasshoppers with huge, long feelers.

The black field cricket is a strange musician — it sings by rubbing its wing casings together and hears with an ear in its front leg.

The green stink bug is true to its name — as you'll find out when you disturb it.

The yellow ambushbug hides in goldenrod flowers where it really does ambush and eat flies and bees that land nearby.

The bee assassin stabs honey bees in the back with its beak while they feed.

The praying mantis looks like it's praying, but it's really preying.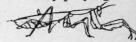

Meadows are often home to the beautiful large black and yellow garden spider.

SPIDER **POWER**

Scientists believe the dry silk made by the orb-weaving spider may be the strongest fibre on Earth. They are looking into reproducing it to make bullet-proof vests, armoured vehicles and boat hulls.

Take care not to damage spider webs. Spiders eat their old webs to help make the silk for spinning new ones. That's recycling for you!

RAISE A MONARCH BUTTERFLY

In a summer meadow where there are milkweed plants, look for a monarch butterfly caterpillar. It's very distinctive with its narrow black, yellow and white stripes. If you have a couple of weeks to care for the creature, here's how you can witness the remarkable change from monarch caterpillar to butterfly.

You'll need:

a large glass jar

milkweed leaves

waxed paper

an elastic band

a fork

1.

Look for a caterpillar about as big as your little finger. Collect the caterpillar and the top of its plant in your glass jar. Put in a few extra milkweed leaves. Cover the jar with waxed paper and secure it with an elastic band. Punch small air holes in the waxed paper with a fork.

2.

Place the bottle outside where it's sheltered from direct sun and from rain (but not where it's damp and miserable, like under the cottage).

3.

Now watch — but don't bump — the bottle. After a few days, the caterpillar will stop moving and hang still under the lid or one of the leaves. Don't worry, nothing is wrong — the caterpillar is spinning its green case, called a chrysalis.

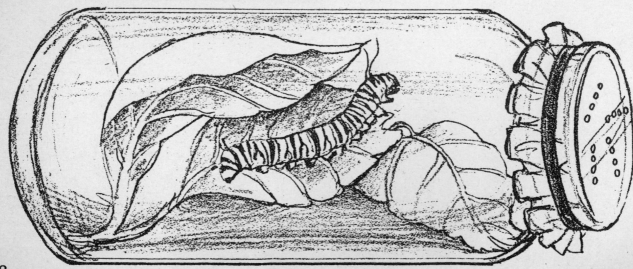

4.

When the chrysalis is finished, take the cover off the jar and gently ease the milkweed part way out so the chrysalis is in the open air. Check every morning and remember to count its golden spots. Before long, the chrysalis will lose its beautiful green and turn dull and dark. When that happens, it's not dying, it's changing again. You should start visiting more often.

5.

When the chrysalis eventually turns clear, with black and orange showing through, stay nearby. The butterfly inside will soon crack the chrysalis. Then the wings will emerge, followed by the whole butterfly. Let it take its time to stretch and dry before flopping away. Look carefully — what's happened to the golden spots?

MONARCH MIGRATION

Did you know that monarch butterflies migrate south for the winter, just like birds do? In the autumn, they fly to southern California and Mexico. There they hang on trees by the millions and doze the winter through. In spring, the females travel to the southern states where they lay their eggs. Those eggs hatch and the adults go farther north to lay eggs again. By the time you see a monarch in the summer, it may be the great-great-grandchild of one that left your meadow for last year's 3000-km (1865-mile) trip south.

SUMMER BIRD FEEDERS

Hanging bird feeders around your cottage is a great way to see birds up close. Here are three summer bird feeders that are easy to make. See how many different kinds of birds you can attract to your feeders.

SEED FEEDER

You'll need:
a clean cardboard milk or juice carton

scissors

string

bird seed

1.
Punch a hole in the centre of the front of your milk carton with scissors and cut out the two sides and the top of a square.

2.
Bend the cut piece out at the bottom and snip it off, leaving a short flap for a perch. Repeat for the opposite side of the carton.

3.
Make a hole through the top of the milk carton with the scissors and thread string through it.

4.
Fill the carton with bird seed and hang your feeder from a tree limb where you can keep an eye on it. Make sure it's well off the ground, but where you can still reach it for refilling. Look for seed-eaters such as rose-breasted grosbeaks and purple finches at your summer seed feeder.

FRUIT FEEDER

You'll need:

- a hammer
- a strong nail
- a piece of partly eaten or spoiled fruit (peach, apple, plum)

1.
Hammer the nail into the side of a tree, above eye level, in a sunny spot you can easily see. Hammer it part way in so the nail is stuck, but it still stands out from the tree.

2.
Punch a piece of fruit onto the nail so it won't fall off.

3.
In the summer's heat, the fruit will start to rot and collect fruitflies. Some birds will come to eat the flies buzzing around the fruit. Others will pick at the fruit itself. When you find another piece of spoiled fruit, jab it onto the nail, too. Look for northern orioles and warblers at your fruit (and fly) feeder.

BIRD FEEDERS AT NIGHT

Don't forget to check all your feeders at night. You may find flying squirrels, luna moths, raccoons, whip-poor-wills and other night-loving creatures helping themselves.

NECTAR FEEDER

You'll need:

- red ribbon
- a clear, long, thin bottle without a lid (an empty medicine bottle works well)
- 50 mL (1/4 cup) sugar
- 250 mL (1 cup) hot water
- red food colouring (optional)
- garbage bag tie

1.
Tie the red ribbon around the neck of your bottle (hummingbirds are attracted to the colour red).

2.
Add 50 mL (1/4 cup) of sugar to 250 mL (1 cup) hot tap water. Stir to dissolve and let the mixture cool.

3.
Pour the sugar and water nectar into the bottle. Add red food colouring to the water if you want. (Leftover nectar can be kept covered in the fridge for refills.)

4.
With the garbage bag tie, wire the bottle to the top of a strong plant or shrub in a sunny spot you can easily see. If you have a patch of red, orange or pink flowers, wire your feeder near them. Look for ruby-throated hummingbirds hovering at your nectar feeder if you live in the east and rufous humming-birds if you live in the west.

81

BIRD BATH

HUMMINGBIRD BATH

If you make the hummingbird feeder on page 81, you'll attract these fascinating little birds. See if they'll drop in for a bath or a drink, too. Use the largest carrot or parsnip you can find.

You'll need:

a penknife
a large carrot or parsnip
a vegetable peeler
a hammer
a thin nail
a toothpick
plastic thread or fine string
water

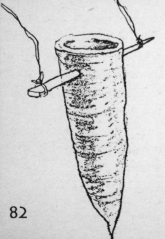

1.
Cut off about 5 cm (2 inches) from the fat end of a carrot. Hollow out the cut end using the end of a vegetable peeler and a penknife.

2.
Gently make a small hole in each side of the carrot with the hammer and nail. Slide the toothpick through the holes, creating a perch.

3.
Tie a piece of thread to each end of the toothpick.

4.
Tie your tiny bath to the branch of a tree, preferably beside a hummingbird feeder.

5.
Fill the carrot regularly with water. Watch and wait for the buzzing thank-you from the hummingbird.

GARBAGE-LID

An old garbage-can lid is the right depth to attract larger birds such as sparrows and robins. If you have a metal one, you can paint it brown or green or just leave it as is. Choose a location that is away from paths but close enough to the cottage for you to see any bird bathers.

You'll need:

a garbage-can lid
sand or an old tire
bricks or large stones

1.
Place the lid on either an old tire or sand (loose dirt). Adjust it so it's level.

BATH

2.

Surround the lid with beach stones or old bricks. This will keep the bath in place and provide landing perches for the birds.

3.

Fill the lid daily with fresh water. Rinse it out with the hose once a week to keep the tin from getting slimy.

THE WATERING HOLE

This bottle bath is mounted on a deck or fence to attract passers-by such as swallows, martins, meadowlarks and bluebirds.

You'll need:

a large pop bottle

a piece of two-by-four slightly taller than your bottle

a pencil

a hammer

4 nails

6 large elastic bands

a fence or deck post

a large margarine or yoghurt tub

1.

Lay your bottle on the wide side of the two-by-four. With your pencil, mark 4 cm (1½ inches) down from the top and again around the fattest part of the bottle. Do the same on the other side.

2.

Hammer the 4 nails into these spots. Hammer in part way, leaving 2 cm (¾ inch) of nail sticking out.

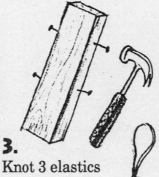

3.

Knot 3 elastics together, then knot the other 3 together.

4.

Check with an adult first, and then nail the two-by-four to a fence or deck post.

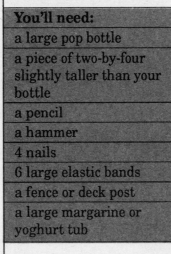

5.

Place the margarine tub, filled with 250 mL (1 cup) of water, on top of the post. Fill the pop bottle with water and hold your hand over the top. Invert the filled bottle into the tub. Attach it to the two-by-four by looping each elastic around the nail on one side, across the bottle and around the nail on the other side.

6.

To refill, remove and fill the bottle. Add more water to the tub, too. Rinse out the bottle and the tub once a week to keep the water clean.

BUILD A BIRD HOUSE

Just as different kinds of birds look different, they like different nests and nesting sites. Here's an easy bird house to make that will suit a bluebird, a tree swallow, a flicker or a house wren.

You'll need:

a large plastic vinegar or bleach bottle (half size for wrens)

muddy water

a sharp knife

small stones

coarse sandpaper

brown exterior house-type paint and a paintbrush

length of wire to tie the house to a tree or post

1.

Wash out the plastic bottle thoroughly. Make a mixture of muddy water with gravel and swirl it around inside the bottle and pour it out again. This will take away the chemical smell and leave a rougher, more natural surface on the inside.

2.

Turn the bottle upside-down and ask an adult to help you cut a circular hole on one side with your knife. The hole should be well above the neck of the bottle. The hole size determines the kind of birds you'll attract (see the list on the next page).

3.

Drop a few stones through that hole until they collect in the neck of the bottle.

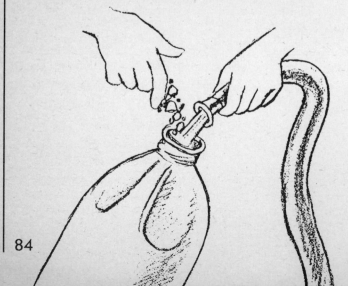

84

4.
Make two small air holes on the sides above the entrance hole.

5.
Using coarse sandpaper, scratch all over the outside of the bottle so paint will stick to it.

6.
Paint the outside of the bird house a light brown colour to make it look like wood. Don't paint the neck of the bottle. While the paint is still wet, carry the bottle to a wooded area and roll it in leaf and twig litter until some has stuck to the paint.

7.
When the paint is dry, run wire through the air holes and out the back. Strap the house to a tree or post and at a height favoured by your chosen bird (see the list below). Remove the cap for drainage.

BIRD HOUSE FACTS

Kind of Bird	Hole Size	Nesting Location
bluebird	4 cm (1 ½ inches)	about 1.5 m (5 feet) off the ground on a post in open country about 10 m (32 feet) from a tree
tree swallow	5 cm (2 inches)	a little higher off the ground than for a bluebird and near a pond
flicker	7-8 cm (3 inches)	about 5 m (16 feet) up a tree trunk on a woodland edge
house wren	3 cm (1 inch)	on the trunk of a thick shrub about 1 m (3 feet) off the ground; house wrens like two houses, one for the young, one for extra nesting materials

PURPLE MARTIN APARTMENT HOUSE

With the help of an adult, you can construct a purple martin apartment house.

1.

Make 6 or more plastic-bottle bird houses as described on page 84, except work with each plastic bottle right-side-up, lid screwed on.

2.

Cut a 5-cm (2-inch) entrance hole for each unit.

3.

Don't drop stones into the neck. Instead, make a few small nail holes in the bottom of the bottle so any rainwater will drain away.

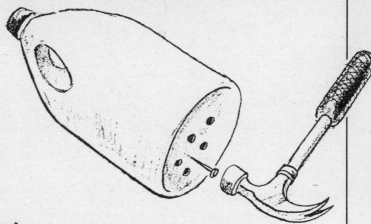

4.

Hang the houses in threes along a wooden bar using wire.

5.
With your adult helper, nail the wooden bars on top of a pole at a height of 3 m (10 feet) or up to 7 m (23 feet).

Purple martins like an open yard away from trees and buildings but near a pond or lake so they can feast on insects such as mosquitoes. Set up your martin apartment late in the summer and you may have a busy colony of families when you return to the cottage next summer. Pioneers believed that if they sprinkled broken eggshells under a martin house, it was more likely to be chosen as a colony house. Why not try it, too?

NATURE BREAK

In 1884, a man actually counted the number of times adult martins in a colony visited their young with food in one day. He counted 3277 visits. When purple martins move into your colony, try sitting outside in the evening to see if you get bothered by mosquitoes. People who have martins near their cottages often say they are never bothered by bugs — the martins have eaten them all.

COUNTING SNAKES

Counting snakes can be fun. How many different kinds can you count? How many of each kind? Your observations and totals can help scientists doing research.

Scientists collect the numbers of snakes sighted over a large region and compile an atlas with the results. Their totals include records of every time an observer spots a snake or good evidence that a snake was recently there — such as a shedded skin or bodily remains. They map out all the snake sightings. By comparing the numbers year to year, they can see which snakes are doing well, which ones are in trouble, and where endangered snakes have been seen so they can be protected.

If you want to help make a snake atlas, count all the snakes you see over the summer. At each sighting, note what kind it was, where you saw it, what time of day it was and any other details you notice. Then, send your information to the scientists who collect sightings from all over the province or state to compile their snake atlas. If you prefer, you can also help track frogs, toads, turtles, birds, mammals or plants.

Here is how you can become an atlaser:

1.
Go to the library and get a field guide to identify different kinds of snakes. Learn to recognize dangerous snakes.

2.
Find out who's compiling the atlas on snakes in your area. Try the local naturalists' club, natural history museum or Ministry of Natural Resources.

3.
Make out several cards like this:

My Name:

Address:

Date of Sighting:

Exact Location:

Type of Snake:

Weather/Time of Day:

Habitat:

What the Snake Was Doing:

4.
Every time you spot a snake, fill out a card.

5.
At the end of the summer, mail all the cards you've collected to your local snake atlas compilers. Ask them to add your records to the provincial or state atlas.

IF YOU SEE A RATTLESNAKE OR OTHER POISONOUS SNAKE, STAY AWAY FROM IT.

S N A K E   F A C T S

- Most mammals and birds are born in springtime, but snakelets emerge well into the summer — the best time for holiday observation. Many snakes lay eggs, but the garter snake and the water snake give birth to live young.

- One female garter snake usually gives birth to about 20 snakelets, but the record is 87. The young are more than 12 cm (5 inches) long at birth. A Canadian water snake may give birth to 30 to 40 live snakelets, but American varieties can produce up to 100 — that's one bellyful!

- The northern water snake can grow to be 1 m (3 feet) long. It may look dangerous and hungry swimming across the waterfront, but it'll turn tail and swim away if you clap or splash. However, big ones will give a nasty bite if you grab at them and try to pick them up.

- As a snake grows, it sheds its outer skin and replaces it with a new one. Look for the leftover skin caught between logs or rocks. A snake works its old skin off, starting at the lips, and leaves it behind all in one piece — but inside-out. The shed skin is see-through, with no colour, but you can make out the pattern of the scales and even the eyeballs.

- When a snake sticks its tongue out at you, it's not being threatening or rude. The snake is only trying to get a sense of what you are. Snakes smell with their forked tongue as well as with their nostrils.

GARDEN GONE WILD

You can attract some wildlife to your cottage by creating a wild garden. By collecting and sowing seeds or transplanting a few plants, you can create a garden full of interesting flowers. You'll have fun watching what comes to eat and visit your garden.

Select your wild spot with an adult's help. It should be out in the open, sunny and fairly flat. A perfect place is where grasses and weeds already grow.

In late summer, explore near your cottage. Take along small, dry containers such as yoghurt tubs or washed-out milk bags. Look for plants that have gone to seed. That means they've finished flowering and are ripening seeds for next year's flowers. Collect a variety of plants and put each type in its own labelled container. A field guide to wild plants will help you identify what you collect.

Here are some seed-producing plants that are easy to collect and are found in most cottage areas.

MILKWEED

Milkweed starts out the summer with pinky purple flowers, then develops a broccoli-like fruiting body, followed by a seed pod bursting with white fluffy parachutes. If you want to attract monarch butterflies or monarch beetles to your wild garden, collect the brown seeds attached to the end of the parachutes.

SEEDS

HOLLYHOCKS

Hollyhocks attract bees, humming-birds, even moths. The seeds ripen in late August in a pod that looks like a dried fig. Many seeds are packed inside a tight circular ring. When they're very dry, they can be flicked out of the ring for planting.

QUEEN ANNE'S LACE

Queen Anne's lace, or wild carrot, attracts beetles such as ladybugs. You can collect the seeds from Queen Anne's lace at the end of the summer. The flower rolls itself up into a dry ball that looks like a small bird's nest. Collect the entire "nest."

SUNFLOWERS

When ripe, in the fall, the middle of the sunflower becomes a dinner plate, attracting blue jays, cardinals, orioles, chipmunks, squirrels, rabbits and raccoons. Check around a bird feeder for a sunflower seed if you can't find a plant growing in the wild.

PREPARING YOUR SEEDS

The seeds of most wild northern plants need to dry out and freeze before they will start to grow in the spring. So you'll have to simulate both an autumn and winter spent on the ground to get your seeds ready for planting. Here's how:

1.
Place each variety of seed on a separate sheet of newspaper to dry in the sun.

2.
Store the dried seeds in yoghurt cups until late August or September.

3.
Place each seed or nut variety in its own labelled jar and cover with a handful of slightly damp peat moss. Screw the lids on tightly.

4.
Place the jars in the shed or pump house — anywhere that's cool and out of the way. The seeds will hibernate and be ready to plant in your wild garden in early spring.

MORE

SPRING PLANTING

As soon as you get to the cottage in late May or in June, get your seed jars out of the shed (see page 91) and plant your wild garden.

1.
Prepare a soil mound for each variety of seeds. With a shovel, dig an area about 50 cm (20 inches) around. Turn the soil over and break it up with the back of the shovel. If you have any compost, now is the time to dig it in. Compost will loosen the soil and add nourishment.

2.

Leave at least a metre (3 feet) between each mound.

3.

Using a stick, poke holes 10 cm (4 inches) deep in the mound, 10 cm (4 inches) apart. Drop a seed into each hole and cover it with soil.

4.

Water the seeds gently and thoroughly.

ECOWATCH

Collect only as many seeds as you need for your wild garden. Ten or twelve seeds of each variety should be enough. You don't want to cause a local extinction, so never take all the seeds from a patch of wildflowers. Then the patch will keep growing next year, too. Always ask permission before you collect seeds from private property. Never take seeds or pick plants from a park or a protected area. Don't buy packs of mixed wild seeds. They often contain seeds of plants that are not local to your cottage and can take over from the native plants.

A BEAUTIFUL KILLER

Purple loosestrife is a beautiful killer. It's not a native plant and it has no natural enemies. Not one North American animal feeds on its leaves, stems or roots. Purple loosestrife is taking over wetlands and waterways, endangering the native plants. Once the native plants are gone, the local wildlife leaves or starves. Each plant can produce up to 2.7 million seeds in just one year, so it spreads like wildfire. Don't plant it in your wild garden. Here's how to identify purple loosestrife: purple or pink flower spikes that bloom from June to September, a woody, square stalk that stands from 1 to 2 m (3 to 7 feet) high, with smooth-edged leaves attached right onto the stalk.

SPYING INTO AN ANTHILL

Have you ever left a picnic lunch on the ground and returned to find your sandwich being carried off by ants? Next time, follow that food back to the anthill. You can construct your own anthill to get an inside look at their busy lives.

You'll need:
- a large clear plastic pop bottle
- a hand saw
- a rectangular-shaped rock, a bit smaller than the bottle
- plastic wrap
- sticky tape
- a tray
- a trowel or large spoon
- a plastic bag
- a pail
- a piece of paper
- a small piece of wet sponge
- a cotton ball
- a small piece of fine fabric
- an elastic band
- an old towel

1.
Ask an adult to help you cut the bottom off your plastic pop bottle with the saw.

2.
Turn the bottle top-side-down and put the rock inside the bottle as shown. The rock will fill the centre of the bottle and force the ants to construct their nests and tunnels against the walls of the bottle where you can see them working.

3.
Stretch plastic wrap over the bottom opening and tape it there so it forms a complete seal.

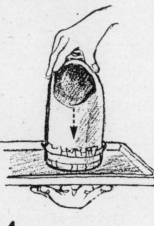

4.
Centre the tray face down on the bottom of the bottle. Holding the neck of the bottle with one hand and pushing on the bottom of the tray with the other hand, turn the bottle right-side-up so that it is sitting in the middle of the tray.

5.
Carry the trowel, plastic bag and pail to your local anthill.

6.
Cut deep into the top of the hill with your trowel. Gently catch some of the scurrying ants in your plastic bag. Search for ants carrying cocoons — they look like pieces of dry rice. Look for a queen ant, too — she'll have a much larger body than regular worker ants.

When you've collected about 20 ants, tie the top of the bag shut. Collect some of the earth from the anthill in your pail. You'll need enough to fill more than half your pop bottle.

7.
Return to your pop bottle. Make a funnel with the piece of paper and pour the earth into the bottle so it falls around the rock.

8.
Poke the piece of wet sponge into the bottle neck and down onto the top of the earth.

9.
Drop in some crumbs from your picnic for good measure.

10.
Pour the ants from the collecting bag in next and quickly poke a cotton ball in the neck after them.

11.
Cover the top of the bottle with a piece of fabric held in place with the elastic band.

12.
Drape the towel over the whole bottle and leave it in darkness.

13.
Once a day take off the towel, open the top and refresh the food supply. Add a few water drops to the sponge. Check to see if the ants have done any construction.

14.
After about 3 days you should start to see tunnels and rooms as if you were looking into an anthill. You should see where they take their food and how they tend their young.

15.
After a couple of weeks of spying on your ants, carry your tray back to the original anthill and rip the plastic off the bottom of the bottle. Let the ants return to their relatives — and to their hard work, including picnic-robbing.

ANT FOOD

You know ants like picnics. But what are their preferred foods? Try giving your ants a small bit of cereal, a shredded piece of meat, a few seeds of grass, a few grains of sugar and so on. Which do they gobble up first? You may be surprised!

95

ANIMAL CLUES

You don't have to see an animal to know that it has visited your property. Animals leave behind clues that clearly say "I've been here." So be a detective and find the clues that tell you who has visited.

RACCOON

Overturned garbage, pilfered compost, crayfish remains on the beach all indicate that the masked bandit has dined nearby. Raccoon paw prints look like tiny human hands.

SKUNK

If your nose doesn't tell you, your lawn will. Holes and rolled-up grass show where the skunk's sharp claws have scrounged a meal of grubs and insects.

DEER

Look for flattened grass in meadows or woodland clearings. You've had a sleep-over guest. Check under apple trees, too — deer love apples for breakfast.

SQUIRREL

The log pile is a good hide-out for a squirrel, mouse or chipmunk. If you find pine cones that have been eaten clean, you have a tenant.

PLASTER-CAST ANIMAL TRACKS

You can make a "negative" impression plaster cast of a bird or animal track. They make pretty impressive doorstops or paper-weights.

You'll need:

heavy cardboard 5 cm x 20 cm (2 inches x 8 inches)
a paper clip
water
a margarine tub
Polyfix or other wall plaster
a stick

1.
Find a clear animal or bird track in mud or sand.

2.
Form the cardboard into a circle, securing it with a paper clip. Place the cardboard around the track and push it gently into the soil or sand.

3.
Pour enough water into the margarine tub to half fill the cardboard mould. Add the plaster a little at a time, stirring with a stick until smooth. The mixture should be as thick as pancake batter. It should pour but not be too runny.

4.
Pour the plaster into the mould.

5.
Let it set for several hours until it's very hard. Drying time will depend on how thick your cast is and the dampness in the air.

6.
Remove the plaster cast from the ground, removing the cardboard mould. Dust off any loose dirt.

7.
You can paint the track or leave it white.

97

FLY A KITE

There's nothing like the feel of a kite pulling up and away from your grip on a windy day. Why not make a kite so you're ready when steady breezes blow?

You'll need:

a felt-tip pen

a tape measure

2 straight sticks or dowelling, about 5 mm (¼ inch) thick and about 70 cm (28 inches) long

1 m (3 feet) fishing line

40 m (130 feet) strong, thin (1 mm) nylon cord

4 straight pins

a piece of light cotton about 80 cm x 80 cm (32 inches x 32 inches)

scissors

white glue

coloured tissue paper

a metal pop can opening tab

a flat wooden stick about 15 cm (6 inches) long

1.
Start by making the frame. With a felt-tip pen, mark a point 20 cm (8 inches) from the end of one stick and then mark a point 35 cm (14 inches) from the end of the other stick. Form a cross with the two sticks so they meet at your two marks. Wind the fishing line crosswise around the joint and knot securely.

2.
Cut off about 4.5 m (15 feet) of the nylon cord. Pin one end of the cord into the bottom tip of the frame. Stretch the cord around the frame and pin it at the other three tips. Bring it back to the bottom and secure it with the first pin. Leave the remaining cord attached to form the kite tail.

3.
Lay the completed frame on the cotton fabric and cut out the kite shape, leaving an extra 2 cm (¾ inch) all around. Snip little "v's" out of each point of the shape.

4.
Spread glue over the 2-cm (¾ inch) margin you left and then fold and press it back over the frame.

5.

To finish off the tail, cut the tissue paper into strips about 30 cm x 15 cm (12 inches x 6 inches). Fold the strips in half lengthwise. Tie the middle of the strips to the tail string of the kite, spacing them about 15 cm (6 inches) apart.

6.

Now it's time to string the kite. Cut 120 cm (47 inches) of cord, fold it in half, push the loop end through the pop-can ring and then slip the loose ends back through the loop. Open up the cord and tie one end to the top of the kite spine and the other to the bottom.

7.

Tie one end of the remaining nylon cord to the flat wooden stick. Wind the cord around and around until you come to the other end. Tie that to the pop-can ring. Now you have your kite attached to its line and you're ready to fly the kite.

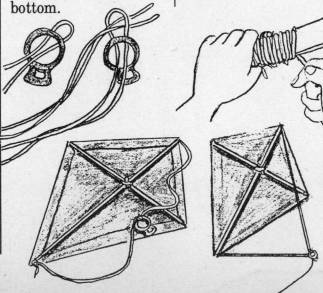

TIPS FOR SUCCESSFUL KITE FLYING

Choose a clear day with a steady wind to try out your kite. Gusty days are hard for beginners. Stand in a place where the wind will blow your kite away from any hydro wires or kite-eating trees.

Let out a few metres (several feet) of the kite line. Ask a friend to toss the kite high in the air while you run the other way, into the wind, letting out line as you go.

If the kite keeps nose-diving, add cord to lengthen the tail. If it keeps falling backward, shorten the tail.

On a calm day, try flying your kite from a motor boat.

NEVER FLY A KITE DURING A THUNDER STORM!

Remember, never fly kites near power lines because you can get electrocuted.

CRAZY KITES

Before you glue on your swatch of light cotton fabric, try painting crazy animal faces or insect bodies on it. Your kite could look like a snarling cat, a lovely butterfly or a monster mosquito.

JUGGLE BUBBLES

Touch a bubble and it bursts, right? Try making the bubble mixture below, and with careful handling you can make bubbles that last a little longer. It's best to do this outside, unless you like mopping floors.

BUBBLE SOLUTION

You'll Need:

50 mL (¼ cup) of dish detergent (Joy works well)
175 mL (¾ cup) of cold water
5 drops of glycerin

Why do bubbles burst? It's because the water in the bubble solution evaporates in the air and the bubbles dry out. Pop. The glycerin in this mixture slows down this process, helping the bubbles last longer.

BUBBLE BLOWERS

Make your own bubble blowers using wire and pliers. A thin coat hanger easily bends into a small circle with a handle. Make other shapes — diamonds, figure eights and squares. Your cutlery drawer may contain ready-made bubble blowers. Try a potato masher, plastic bottle cap, slatted spoon, apple corer, plastic straw...

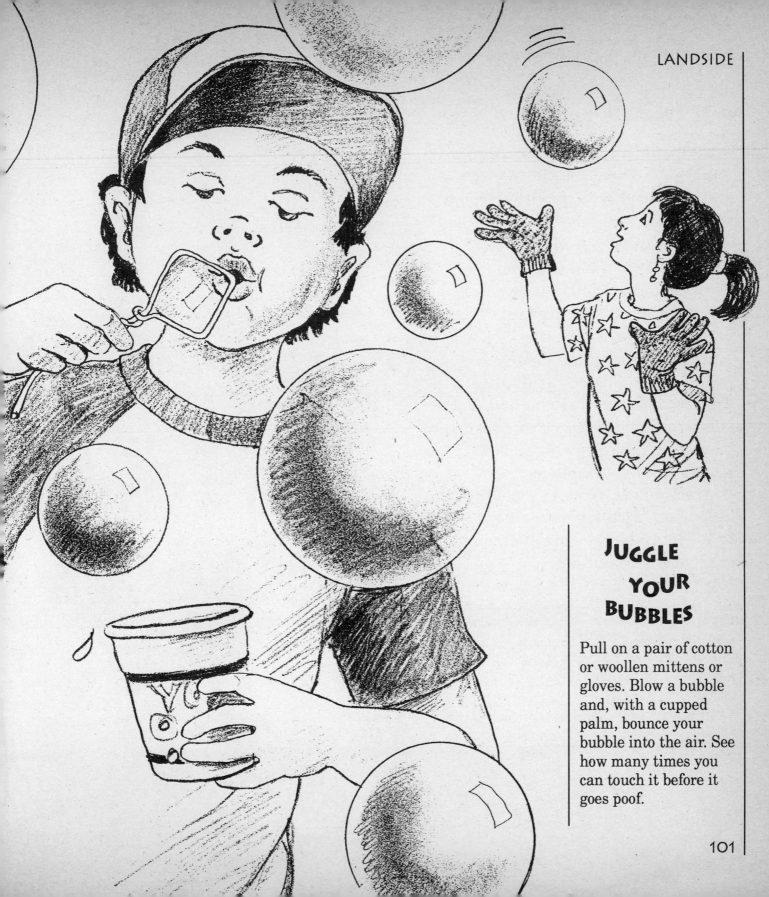

JUGGLE YOUR BUBBLES

Pull on a pair of cotton or woollen mittens or gloves. Blow a bubble and, with a cupped palm, bounce your bubble into the air. See how many times you can touch it before it goes poof.

TREE FORT

If you build a tree fort this summer, you'll have a spot to call your own. You'll enjoy sharing it with a friend or with a book.

Think about the location of your tree fort. You'll want to hear the dinner call, but be far enough away to feel private. Look for a tree with lower branches about 1.5 m (5 feet) off the ground. It's difficult and dangerous to build too high up in the tree. One solid sturdy tree, or a clump of smaller trees growing close together, will support your hide-out.

Once you've picked a location, become an architect and design your fort. Then, change hats and become a carpenter and build it.

You'll need:
an adult helper
a measuring tape
a pencil
paper
scrap wood
a hand saw
a hammer
5-cm (2-inch) nails
10-cm (4-inch) nails
a drill

1.
With a measuring tape, pencil and paper, climb the tree to the first main branches. (Use a ladder if necessary, with the help of an adult.)

2.
Measure the distance between the branches.

3.

Draw a rough layout of the floor plan. You may find that a triangular or quadrilateral shape will fit neatly on top of the lower branches. You can adjust the floor later if it's uneven.

4.

Look around your property for wood. You'll need two-by-fours for the frame and the railings, and a sheet of plywood or planks for the floor boards and railings.

5.

The frame pieces should extend beyond the tree trunk. It is better to cut the pieces too long and trim them later than cut them too short. Using your sketch to guide you, measure the two-by-four and mark with a pencil.

6.

Ask an adult to help you saw 3 or 4 pieces to form the frame for the floor. Nail them together using 5-cm (2-inch) nails.

7.

Your adult helper will have to help you hoist the frame up into the tree. Avoid pruning or cutting off branches — they provide more privacy.

8.

If the floor frame is not level, slide an extra piece of wood under the side that is too low.

9.

Hammer the frame securely into place, using 10-cm (4-inch) nails.

10.

If you're using planks for the floor boards, use your sketch to help you determine how many boards you'll need and what length they should be. Not all the floor boards will be the same length. Plan ahead so you don't waste wood. Use your measuring tape and pencil to mark the planks.

11.

Saw the planks to the right length. Lay them onto the frame, leaving a small gap between each board for drainage. Nail the floor boards onto the frame, using 5-cm (2-inch) nails.

12.

If you have a piece of plywood, use a pencil and ruler to draw the dimensions of the floor on the wood. Using a saw, cut the plywood to fit. Using a drill or a large nail and hammer, make drainage holes in the floor. Nail the board in place using 5-cm (2-inch) nails.

It is better to have no
railing than a wobbly
one. To make it secure,
you'll need to brace the
top and bottom of the
railing with pieces of
two-by-four. Decide
which three sides of
your fort to rail in,
then proceed to make
the railing as follows:

13.

Measure 30 cm (1 foot) and 60 cm
(2 feet) up from the floor of the
fort. Mark the tree trunk with a
pencil.

14.

Cut 6 pieces of two-by-four to form a frame for
the railing. Nail them into the tree trunk at the
pencil marks, using 10-cm (4-inch) nails.

15.

Cut planks into 60-cm (2-foot) lengths. Nail them
on the outside of the fort to the two-by-four
frame, using 5-cm (2-inch) nails.

If your fort is too high off the ground to climb up
easily, turn to page 55 and make a Tarzan rope
to help you scale the tree trunk. Pull the rope up
after you if you want to control who gets to come
into the fort.

The construction of your fort is now complete,
but you may want to add some finishing touches.
Turn the page for some neat ideas.

FORT DECOR

Here are some ideas to jazz up your tree fort (see page 102).

PERSONALIZED SIGN

Give your fort a name and post it on a sign.

You'll need:

a permanent marker or outdoor paint

plywood board about 30 cm x 15 cm (12 inches x 6 inches)

a hammer

5-cm (2-inch) nails

1.

Choose a name for your fort. It can include your own name, such as Robbie's Roost or Ellen's Aerie. You can simply write "Kids Only" or "Private Property."

2.

Write or paint the name of the tree fort on the board.

3.

Hammer your sign up near the entrance of the fort. Nail it into the wooden part of the fort, not the tree trunk.

BASEBALL HOLDER

You'll need:

a small tin can

a hammer

5-cm (2-inch) nails

1.

A tuna-fish or cat-food can is the right size to hold a baseball. Using the hammer, smooth the edge where the lid was removed.

2.

Choose a spot for your holder. You'll need to nail it into a two-by-four.

3.

Nail the tin so that it is straight. Voilà! You'll always be able to find your baseball when you want to play catch.

FIRE FIGHTER'S POLE

When the dinner bell goes or there are too many mosquitoes in your fort, here's a great way to make a speedy exit.

You'll need:

a shovel

a long piece of plumbing tube 15 cm (6 inches) in diameter

1 bag of cement

bungy cord or cord for lashing

1.
Locate your fire fighter's pole where there is a clear drop to the ground, away from tree branches and shrubs. You'll need to secure the top of the pole in a branch higher up in the tree, above the fort.

2.
Dig a hole about 1 m (3 feet) deep.

3.
Place the plumbing tube in the hole and wedge the top in branches above the fort, close to the tree trunk.

4.
Mix the cement according to the directions on the package. Pour it into the hole. Allow the cement to dry around the pole.

5.
Pack dirt on top of the cement.

6.
Secure the top of the pole with a bungy cord or rope by tying the pole to the trunk of the tree. Ask an adult to check that the pole is stable.

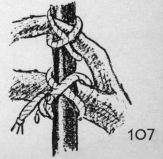

107

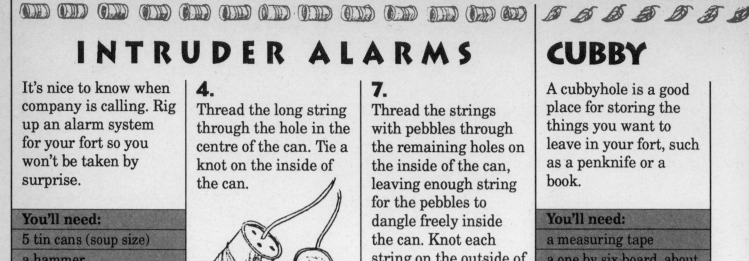

INTRUDER ALARMS

It's nice to know when company is calling. Rig up an alarm system for your fort so you won't be taken by surprise.

You'll need:

5 tin cans (soup size)
a hammer
a large nail
string
scissors
15 pebbles

1.
Wash the tin cans and remove the labels.

2.
Using a nail, hammer 4 holes in the lid of each can, one in the middle for hanging up your alarm.

3.
For each can cut one hanging string 40 cm (15 inches) long.

4.
Thread the long string through the hole in the centre of the can. Tie a knot on the inside of the can.

5.
For each can, cut three pebble strings, 15 cm (6 inches) in length.

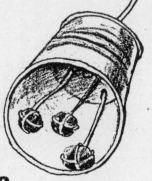

6.
Tie and knot each string around one pebble as you would wrap a parcel.

7.
Thread the strings with pebbles through the remaining holes on the inside of the can, leaving enough string for the pebbles to dangle freely inside the can. Knot each string on the outside of each can.

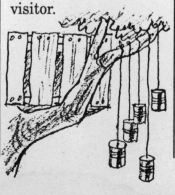

8.
Tie the can to a branch near the entrance to your fort. When the cans ring like a bell, you'll know you have a visitor.

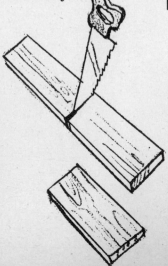

CUBBY

A cubbyhole is a good place for storing the things you want to leave in your fort, such as a penknife or a book.

You'll need:

a measuring tape
a one by six board, about 1m (39 inches) in length
a hand saw
a hammer
5-cm (2-inch) nails

1.
Measure, mark and then saw, two 30-cm (12 inch) pieces of the board. These two pieces will form the bottom and the back of the cubby.

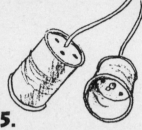

BIRD WATCH

2.

Measure and mark two 15-cm (6-inch) pieces on the board. Draw a line to form a right-angle triangle as shown. Saw these pieces. These two pieces form the ends of the cubby.

3.

Nail the bottom and the back of the cubby together. A nail at each end and two in between should be enough. Then, nail the triangular ends on the cubby.

4.

Choose a spot in the fort for your cubby and nail it in place.

In mid-August, warblers begin their fall migration. If you sit quietly in your fort, you can watch as the warblers flit through in waves. They don't flock and travel large distances in the daytime. They seem to go tree by tree, feeding and chirping along the way. A field guide to birds will help you identify the warblers, but they aren't called "confusing fall warblers" for nothing! In fall they all have similar plumage — mostly olive green, white and yellow. Watch carefully for the subtle differences between them — white wing bars, eye patches or yellow throats.

SECRET COMMUNICATIONS

In the close quarters of the cottage, it's hard to have any privacy. There are times when you want to have a private conversation or send a secret message. Here are two activities that will help you do just that.

SEND A JUICY MESSAGE

You'll need:
- 1 stick
- 15 mL (1 tbsp) lemon juice
- an egg cup
- paper
- a lamp

1.
Find a stick shaped like a pencil.

2.
Pour the lemon juice into the egg-cup "ink well."

3.
Dip the stick "pencil" into the lemon and write your message on a plain sheet of white paper. When the "ink" dries, your page will appear blank.

4.
To de-code the message, hold the paper near a light bulb. The heat from the lamp will cook the lemon and make your secret message turn black. The lemon actually burns, turning to carbon. That is why the message appears black.

CAN-CORD PHONE

You'll need:

a can opener

2 empty small cans

heavy-weight paper bag

a pencil

scissors

2 elastic bands

Vaseline or other petroleum jelly

a darning needle

a long piece of string

1.

Remove the lids of the cans — top and bottom. If the can has sharp edges, ask an adult to help file the edges smooth.

2.

Place your cans on the paper bag and draw circles 5 cm (2 inches) larger than each can. Cut them out, using scissors.

3.

Dampen the papers and wrap them over one end of each can. Hold the paper in place with elastics. These are the receiving ends.

4.

Allow the paper to dry. Now smooth a small amount of Vaseline on the paper. The grease will make the paper stronger.

5.

Thread the darning needle with the string. Pass the needle through the centre of one paper "receiver." Gently make a knot on the inside. Repeat with the second phone. Now you've made the connection and your can-cord phones are ready to use.

Make sure you hold the string taut above the ground, not touching anything. When you speak into your phone, the paper will vibrate and so will the string. When the vibrations (or sound waves) reach the other phone, your voice will be heard in the other phone. Now, those are good vibes!

AFTER DARK

There's lots to do outside
on a summer's night.
Start a bonfire and
swap stories or snuff the
lights and watch a
meteor shower. Maybe
you'd like to prowl and
get to know the nightlife
by the shine in their
eyes. Or learn to
distinguish between the
night calls of frogs and
toads. Read on to find
out how.

CAMPFIRE RING

Why do people like to have a campfire in the summer? For starters it's sometimes cool in the evening, and a fire's warm company. Besides, how else can you roast marshmallows? First you'll need to find a good site for your campfire. Follow the directions below and you'll be having fun by the fire before you know it.

CHOOSING A SITE

Ask an adult to help you choose the location of your fire pit. It's best to place it out in the open. If you have a rocky point, that's ideal. If you have to, you can build a fire pit on the lawn, but you'll have to dig out the grass around it first. Dry grasses and leaves can catch fire. So can overhanging trees, lawn cuttings, bushes and shrubs. Anything too close to the fire pit could accidentally catch fire, so choose your site carefully.

Collect large stones for marking out the edge of the fire pit. Bricks can be used as an alternative. Take time to arrange the rocks neatly and adjust each one, making sure it's not wobbly. Make your fire pit a small, manageable size. The size of a bicycle wheel is big enough. Turn the page to find out how to set your fire.

BUILDING A FIRE

Now you're ready to set your fire in the fire pit. If it's windy, wait for a calmer night to have a fire. If it's been raining and the ground is wet, lay some bark from a dead tree on the bottom of the pit.

Now you need a wood pile. You'll need three sizes of wood: tinder, kindling and fuel.

TINDER

Tinder will flare up and catch fire when you strike a match. Hunt for dead, dry pine needles, birchbark from fallen trees and little twigs. Or make a furze stick (see the box on this page). Place several furze sticks on top with other tinder.

KINDLING

Next, make a tepee shape with the kindling. Kindling burns longer than the "poof" ignition of tinder. From the ground, collect sticks that are as big around or bigger than a pencil. Dry pieces of bark work, too, but don't strip bark off a live tree. Using a match, light the tinder underneath the kindling.

FUEL

Once the kindling is burning well, add fuel. Fuel is what keeps the fire going. You'll need an adult to help you gather a supply of larger logs, as big around as your arm or leg. Most wood lots have a number of fallen trees that can be sawn up into fuel. Never cut down a live tree — use only old, dry wood.

MAKING A FURZE STICK

To make a furze stick, you need a sharp penknife (see the next page for knife safety) and a dry stick that's about the size of a medium carrot. Hold the top of the stick firmly in one hand. With the knife blade pointing away from you, loosen little pieces from the bottom of the stick, without removing them from the stick. Work your way up to the centre of the stick, creating feather-like pieces of wood as thin as a match. Turn the stick the other way around and work your way to the middle again. This way your hand never comes near the blade of the knife.

COOK IN A FIRE PIT

A cooking fire is laid out slightly differently than a comfort fire. Lay the fire between two wet logs or large rocks set slightly apart. Rest a cooking pot on top of the logs.

PUTTING OUT A FIRE

Putting out a fire takes as much care as lighting one. Never leave a fire unattended. When the beans are eaten and the marshmallows are finished, put the fire out — completely. Sprinkle the entire fire pit with water. Stir the ashes, coals and fuel with a long stick and pour on more water. Continue to do this until the fire pit is completely cold. Fire can travel underground along roots, so it's important to double check that the soil under your fire is cold and wet.

KNIFE **SAFETY**

A good knife and a hatchet are essential tools for lighting a fire, but it takes careful practice to learn to use them properly.

Remember, knives are tools, not toys. So choose your tools to last. You won't outgrow them. You'll need a simple folding pocket knife. Extra doodads and gadgets aren't needed. Choose a small, light hatchet.

Look after your knife and hatchet by keeping them clean, dry and sharp. Sharpen them using a drop of oil, such as WD-40, on the blades and rubbing them on a sharpening stone. Stroke the blade away from you at a 20° angle over the sharpening stone. Keep the blade lightly oiled.

Store your knife and hatchet away from younger children. Knives should be closed or in a sheath. Hatchets should be stored with the blade covered.

BONFIRE EVENING

It's a dark and moonless night. The bonfire's crackling and your family and friends are toasting marshmallows. The scene is set for one of your famous ghost stories. Check out the cauldron for the essential ingredients of a spine-tingling tale. Then put a flashlight under your chin to distort your face and make scary shadows.

QUAVERY VOICE

DRAG IT OUT. CREATE SUSPENSE

BLACK CATS, NUMBER 13. WALKING UNDER A LADDER

AWFUL NOISES — SCREAMS, MOANING, OWL HOOTS, DEEP VOICES

BLOODY AXE

SKELETONS

REPETITION

GREEN HANDS, GOLDEN ARMS, BLOODY FINGERS

KNOCK ON THE DOOR

MYSTERIOUS PHONE CALLS

OLD OUTHOUSE

ABANDONED FARM

SHIPWRECK OFF THE POINT

CLAPS OF THUNDER, GUSTS OF WIND

CREAKING DOOR

BRANCHES SCRATCHING ON THE WINDOW

SHOUT OUT THE PUNCH LINE

Here's a sample ghost story you can adapt to your own cottage. Use family names and describe a room in your cottage. Make your family and friends think it could happen to them. Be prepared to leave the light on when you go to sleep tonight!

You are all alone in the cottage. The phone rings, but you decide to answer it anyway. A high-pitched, squeaky voice says, "I'm holding a bloody finger and I'm three doors away." The line goes dead. Your skin begins to crawl. You check all the locks on the cottage doors and windows. Draw the curtains. Listen to the rain on the roof. The phone rings again. The same hideous voice says, "I'm holding a bloody finger and I'm two doors away." Click. The refrigerator squeals to life and you jump out of your chair, hands sweating. RRRRing. "I'm holding a bloody finger and I'm one door away." Click. Your heart is pounding and you dash around wildly. A clap of thunder rocks the cottage. The lights flicker. Suddenly there is a pounding on the door. You know you shouldn't answer but some unnatural force drags you towards the door. You turn the knob, very slowly. Standing on the doorstep is little Ian from down the bay. He holds up his bloody finger and says, "Do you have a bandage?"

CAMPFIRE SINGALONG

After ghost-story telling, you may want to lighten up the mood with a singsong. A good opener is the tried and true "Quartermaster store" song, which you can adapt for the cottage. Here are some ideas to get your imagination started:

"There were loons loons walking like raccoons on the shore on the shore, there were loons loons walking like raccoons on the hot and sandy shore." Or, "There were fleas fleas riding water skis." Or, "There were snakes snakes swimming in the lake."

Make sure you bring in all the voices around the fire and encourage everyone to make up a verse. This is a great cottage tradition to start.

NIGHT LIGHT

The spotlight outside the cottage was put there so you can see in the dark, right? You may not know it, but that light is ideal for attracting night, or nocturnal, creatures. So turn on that outside light and watch.

MOTH MANIA

In early summer, late in the afternoon, smear ripe banana or peanut butter on a tree near the light. Then sit back in the night shadows and wait. You might want to check the tree early in the morning. Do any daytime creatures like banana?

Moths prefer the dark but they'll come to an outdoor light in search of food. Mosquitoes, mayflies and midges will also swarm around the light and attract bigger insect predators. You can even encourage a beautiful lunar moth to visit, so you can check out its huge, smoky, pale green wings. If you attract one to your night light, treat it with respect. They live just a few days — only long enough to mate and lay eggs.

TOAD HOLES

Toads feed at night and will station themselves just beyond an outside light. Their quick tongues dart out and snare unsuspecting insects. Why not make the toad a permanent home and have a natural mosquito controller move in?

You'll need:

a shovel

a 30-cm (12-inch) piece of pipe or weeping tile

a small pail of sand

a handful of gravel-sized rocks

1.
Choose a good location for your toad hole in the sheltered shade just outside the range of your outside light. Beside a stairway is perfect.

BATS

3.
Pour in about 20 cm (8 inches) of sand for drainage. The toad won't want to sit in a puddle after it rains.

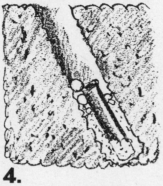

2.
Dig a hole about 80 cm (32 inches) deep and a little bigger around than your pipe. Put the pipe in the hole, angling it a little, as shown.

4.
Drop in a few pebbles and stones for the toad to perch on. Check your toad hole each night to see if a toad has moved in.

In late evening, bats begin their nocturnal activities with a drink from the lake. Then you'll see them swooping near the cottage lights looking for prey. Listen for their high-pitched sounds — clicks, buzzes and cries. They are listening to echoes of their own voices to locate prey and avoid obstacles as they fly.

Some of these sounds you can hear, others are too high-pitched for human ears. If a moth starts to fly in a wild zigzag pattern or if it dive-bombs to the ground to hide in the grass, you'll know there is a bat looking for dinner close by. Turn the page to find out how to build a bat hang-out.

ECOWATCH

Now that you've invited a toad to move in, enjoy watching it but don't handle it. Toads don't give people warts but they do secrete a nasty substance through their skin. It is poisonous to small predators such as weasels, foxes and raccoons. Listen for your toad trilling. Its high, single note is softer and longer than a frog's croaking.

BATS INSIDE

Bats should never be picked up. They can carry rabies and when startled, they will bite. The best way to get a bat out of the cottage is to open all the windows and doors. If this doesn't work, throw a light blanket over the bat and gently take it outdoors. You can discourage bats from nesting in your cottage by caulking cracks in walls and chimneys. Bats can slip through very narrow cracks.

BUILD A BAT HANG-OUT

One bat can eat 500 mosquitoes an hour on a summer's night. Why not make a bat box so you can make use of this remarkable and cheap insect-control service?

You'll need:

a hand saw

a rough, unplaned, untreated plank of wood at least 2 cm (¾ inch) thick and 15 cm (6 inches) wide

a pencil

4 smaller strips of wood, each about 2 cm (¾ inch) wide and 15 cm (6 inches) long

white carpenter's glue

a hammer

nails or screws and screwdriver

tacks

scrap of tarpaper (a dark green plastic garbage bag will also work)

1.
Ask an adult to help you saw a piece of plank about 25 cm (10 inches) long for the backboard.

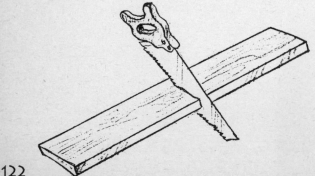

2.
Saw another piece at least 15 cm (6 inches) long for a frontboard. Lay the frontboard on the backboard a few centimetres (1 inch) down from the top and draw a pencil line on the backboard all around where the front sits.

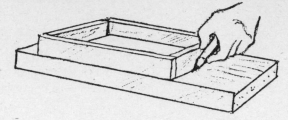

3.
Lay your smaller strips of wood along the pencil line and cut them with the saw so they fit neatly right around. Trim the floor strip about 4 cm (1½ inches) shorter than the length of the bottom and angle it upward to make an entrance.

4.
Glue the side and top strips on edge onto the backboard. Nail or screw them in place. Screw on the bottom strip, but leave it loose so that it can be tilted to clean out the bat box once a year.

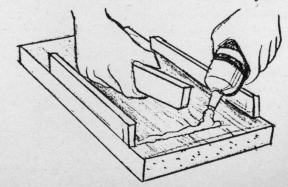

5.

Smear glue along the edge of the top and side strips and lay on the frontboard. Then, nail or screw the frontboard down.

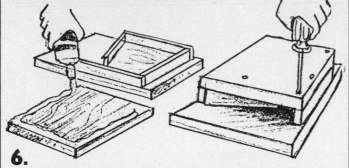

6.

Tack tarpaper on the back of the backboard, pull it over the top and tack it part way down the frontboard.

7.

Now, hang your bat box. Choose a spot sheltered from the wind, on an outside wall or on a tree but away from branches, and facing southwest or southeast so that the inside will get warm in the sun. Your box is best sited near a meadow or pond where night-time mosquito hunting is good. Nail the backboard top and bottom so the entrance is at least 5 m (16 feet) off the ground.

BAT FACTS

- Bats may move into your bat box soon after it's hung — or wait to go house-hunting in early April. Leave your box up over the winter.
- In summer, mother bats like their nest to be toasty warm — 26 to 32°C (80 to 90°F) if possible. Males choose cooler hang-outs away from the young.
- Bats roost by day and fly off to feed at night. Watch your box at dusk to see bats take off.
- Bats are fussy about personal hygiene. They lick their fur, scratch themselves and wipe their faces. They are particularly fussy about keeping their wings clean. Bat poop, called guano, is a great fertilizer for your garden. It will collect under the bat box.
- All cottage-country bats eat only insects. In some parts of the world, bats eat pollen and are important pollinators of fruits. Blood-sucking vampire bats are tropical.
- Bats will leave their nesting spots by September to look for warmer winter hang-outs in hollow trees, caves and the attics of old buildings. They hibernate over winter.

NIGHT PROWL

What goes bump outside in the night? If you really want to know, you can take a night prowl. You'll be surprised at who's making those noises out there.

You'll need:
a red bandanna or scarf
a flashlight
dark clothing (be sure to stay away from roads)
a friend or an adult

1.
Tie the red bandanna over your flashlight so when it's on, the light is still strong but glows red.

2.
Wait for a clear night and put on your dark clothes. Rub dirt on your face and hands, too, if you want to really act the part.

3.
Take a friend and tell an adult where you're going and when you'll be back. Step outside, away from the house lights, and turn on your flashlight.

4.
Stand still to get used to the dark. Look at the trees and watch how moonlight and breezes play on them. Each kind of tree moves in its own way. Maples, for instance, have a darker leaf top than underside so when a breeze passes, the whole tree ripples light and dark like running water.

5.

When you're used to the dark, walk ahead softly. Sweep the dark with your light. When you hear a sound, track it in the flashlight beam.

Here are some of the things you may see and what they likely are:

black, zigzagging shadows in the air	bats
flashes of light in the grass or bushes	fireflies
tiny glowing dots of light on the ground or in rotting logs	beetle grubs or fungus
tiny, crawling specks of white	wolf spider eyes
large, close-set, orange eyeshine	bear — oops — walk away noisily, yelling and throwing things hard on the ground
bright yellow eyeshine	raccoon
shining green eyeshine	bullfrog
bright white eyeshine	dog, coyote or wolf
dull white eyeshine	whip-poor-will
flash of white tails hopping near the ground	cotton-tail rabbit
bounding away above eye-level	white-tailed deer
white streaks waddling along the ground	skunk
a silent shadow gliding tree to tree	owl

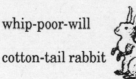

NIGHT OWL

When you hear an owl call, stop and listen for the next round. Count the number of sounds and memorize the rhythm. When you think you've got it, repeat the call several times. The owl may come to investigate, thinking you're another owl trespassing on its territory.

Here are the sounds and rhythms of owl calls you may hear:

HOOTING:

great horned owl
WhaWhaWha - Whooo - Whooo
WhaWhaWhaWha - Whooo - Whooo

barred owl
Whoo - Whoo - WhaWho - Whoohoohoohoaw
(Who cooks, who cooks for you all)

SHRIEKING:

barn owl
Chaaaaaaaaaaaaaaaaaaaaaaaaaaak
(can hiss, too)

long-eared owl
Waaaaaaaaaaaaaaaaaaaaaaaaaaaaaa
(can be wheezy or shrill)

WAILING:

screech owl
Oo-o-o-o-o-o-o-o-o-000000
(descending and quavering like a far-away ghost)

WORM FARM

When you're on your night prowl, why not look for some worms, too? Earthworms can be kept for a few weeks in a jar. All you have to do is duplicate the environment in which they were living and provide them with fresh food and water. The key to success is care. In a few short weeks, you can have a fascinating snarl of tunnels to watch and — if you're lucky — baby worms. At the end of the summer, you can add your worms to your composter and they will help create new soil for next summer's tomatoes.

You'll need:

the largest jar you can find — a 4-L (1-gallon) condiment jar works as well

loose soil

sand

water

leaves

lettuce

a flashlight

4 to 6 worms

a clean yoghurt or margarine container

a brown paper bag

scissors

sticky tape

1.
Fill your jar three-quarters full with layers of loose garden or woodland soil and sand. Do not pack it in. Sprinkle lightly with water. Place several leaves on the top and a few bits of lettuce.

2.
Keep your worm farm in a cool place, such as a shed or basement. Choose a spot away from sunlight and too much heat. Now you're ready to hunt for worms.

3.
Worms can be found easily after a rain or at night using a flashlight. They live in cool, damp places so look under logs, at the edge of a woods or dig in the garden. Collect 4 to 6 worms, along with a handful of soil, in the yoghurt cup.

4.

Place the worms in their prepared home and leave them undisturbed for a few days to let them settle.

5.

Make a protective paper sleeve to slip over the outside of the jar to keep out light and heat. This is easily done with a brown paper bag, scissors and some tape. Make it loose enough so you can slip it off for viewing the worms.

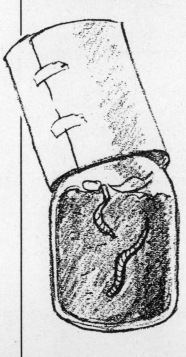

6.

Replace the lettuce leaves every other day.

7.

Return the worms to their original home or add them to your composter when you're finished watching your wormery.

FOOD AND WATER

Worms will eat a variety of garden leaves so try several kinds and note what they like and what they leave behind. You can also use carrot tops, cabbage or lettuce leaves. Remove any rotting food from the jar.

Worms need water, too, but don't want to live in a swamp. Worms breathe through their skin and will drown if the soil is too wet. Keep the soil damp by misting the inside of the jar with a squirt gun or letting a few drops drip from your finger.

WORM WATCHING

Now prepare for some serious worm watching. You will be able to see their tiny hair-like "feet," called setae, as the worms slither up the side of the jar. Are they moist and slimy? Which end is which? The mouth opens and shuts as they move along. Do they ever go backward? Tap on the outside of the jar and see what they do. What does the soil look like after a few days? Have the worms mixed it up into a zigzag of sand and soil?

Worms are blind but they are still sensitive to light. They are nocturnal (active at night), slipping back into the soil by dawn. That's a good way for them to avoid the hunting beaks of robins. Use a flashlight to check on your worm farm at night. Do they react to the light?

Worms are also deaf but they can still sense vibration. When they feel the footfalls of birds or animals, they retreat into their burrows.

STARS IN YOUR EYES

A visit to the country is a great time to go star-gazing. There's so much to see in the sky, and away from city lights, the stars look clearer.

Summer is the best time to see the Milky Way running northeast to southwest across the night sky. There are so many stars in the Milky Way that, in some places, they seem to smudge together. Only in the summer do the constellations Sagittarius and Scorpio peek up over the southern horizon. The biggest yearly display of shooting stars, the Perseid meteor shower, happens in early August. On clear nights, you can trace satellites, watch northern lights dance and even spot the moons of Jupiter.

Here's how you can make a simple reflecting telescope to get a look at summer's star show.

You'll need:

a curved shaving mirror

a small standard flat mirror

a magnifying glass

1.

Stand the shaving mirror so it points at the moon or a star you want to see.

2.

Hold a flat mirror in front of it so you can see the reflection of the shaving mirror in it.

3.

Look into that reflection with the magnifying glass. Everything will look much closer through the magnifying lens.

The familiar, soft face of the moon reveals surprising pocks and ragged lumps through a reflecting telescope.

SHOOTING STAR WATCH

The best way to watch the Perseid meteor shower is to plan a sleep-out on August 10, 11 or 12. These are the nights, each summer, that Earth's orbit passes through a band of space debris that was once released from the trail of a comet when it got too close to the sun. Each piece of debris is hardly bigger than a flake of dust, but when one hits the Earth's atmosphere, it flares into the dazzling arc of light we call a meteor or shooting star — and then it disappears.

Find a comfy spot to lay your blankets where you'll get a view of the whole sky. Then lie back and watch — you'll see about one meteor a minute. When you wake up in the night, check the sky. You'll see more shooting stars after midnight.

SUMMER CONSTELLATIONS

LOOKING NORTH BEFORE MIDNIGHT

- Even though they lived thousands of kilometres (miles) and years apart, both North American Native people and ancient Greeks saw a bear in the stars around the **Big Dipper**. Nowadays, the constellation is called **Ursa Major**, the Great Bear.

- The Big Dipper got its name from a long-handled ladle used to scoop water from a pail in pioneer times. In England, the same star formation is called the Plough or the Wagon.

- Find the **North Star** by following where the Big Dipper pours. If you lie awake overnight and look at the North Star, all the other stars seem to move around it. That's because the Earth rotates on its axis along the same line as the North Star.

- The North Star forms the tip of the handle of the **Little Dipper**, also called **Ursa Minor** or the Little Bear.

- The constellation **Cassiopeia** makes a large, wobbly "W" at the top end of the **Milky Way**.

LOOKING SOUTH BEFORE MIDNIGHT

- People say that **Sagittarius**, at the base of the Milky Way, looks sort of like a teapot. To ancient Greeks, it looked like a centaur — half man, half horse.

- Beside the teapot, the constellation **Scorpius** has the giant red star called **Antares** for a head. Scorpius is so far south, only on very dark, clear summer nights can you see all of the scorpion's body above the horizon.

LOOKING OVERHEAD BEFORE MIDNIGHT

- The **Summer Triangle** is easy to spot because it's made up of three of the brightest stars in the night sky — **Vega**, **Altair** and **Deneb**. Each of these is the main star in its own constellation.

- Vega, the brightest star in the Summer Triangle, forms the centre of the constellation **Lyra**, the Harp.

- Altair, the southern star in the Summer Triangle, is the head of **Aquila** the eagle.

- Deneb is the star head of the **Northern Cross**. The ancient Greeks saw **Cygnus** the swan in the same formation and put Deneb as the swan's tail.

- To the west of the Summer Triangle, look for the small and beautiful **Corona Borealis** or Northern Crown.

- Far to the west is the bright orange star, **Arcturus**. Arcturus is at the foot of a constellation that looks like a kite. The Greeks called the constellation **Bootes**, the Herdsman.

To find constellations in the night sky, look north and hold this book overhead with the page facing down, or look south and turn the diagram upside down.

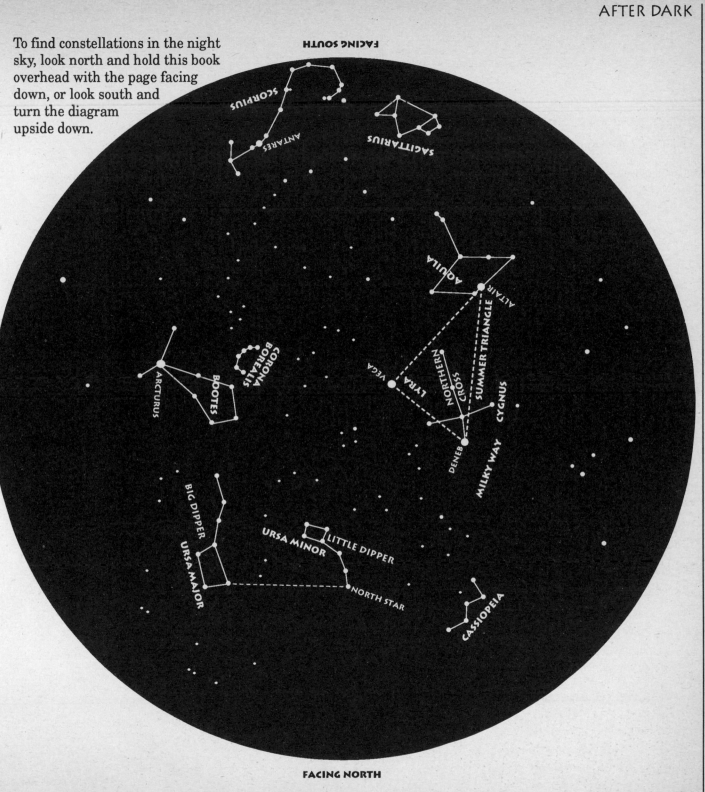

FACING SOUTH

SCORPIUS

ANTARES

SAGITTARIUS

AQUILA

ALTAIR

SUMMER TRIANGLE

CORONA BOREALIS

BOOTES

ARCTURUS

VEGA

LYRA

NORTHERN CROSS

CYGNUS

MILKY WAY

DENEB

BIG DIPPER

URSA MINOR

LITTLE DIPPER

URSA MAJOR

NORTH STAR

CASSIOPEIA

FACING NORTH

131

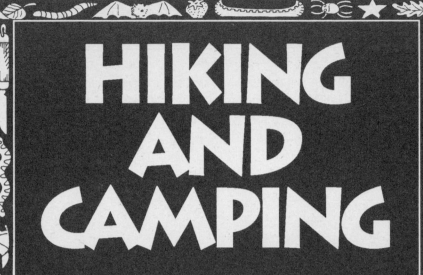

HIKING AND CAMPING

Sometimes it's fun to get away from home base for a while. In this section, you'll learn what to take on a hike and how to plan a cookout. You'll find out how to tell what direction you're travelling in and what to do about poison ivy and mosquitoes. Maybe you'd like to develop wilderness survival skills in case you really need to use them one day. It's all coming up —
just read on.

EXPEDITION SATCHEL

Don't throw away those favourite old jeans. Remodel them to make an expedition satchel. Fill the pockets with hiking essentials so you'll be ready to go when the weather is right.

You'll need:

an old belt or a piece of rope

1 pair of old jeans

2 pieces of old sheet 10 cm (4 inches) wide and 1.5 m (5 feet) long

1.
Insert the belt or rope through the belt loops of the jeans.

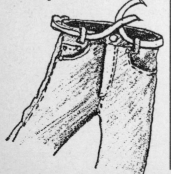

2.
Tie off the bottom of each pant leg with one end of a piece of sheet. Knot them tightly.

3.
Slide the other end of the sheet into the belt loops at the back of the jeans. These tied-off legs form the shoulder straps of the satchel. Adjust the length of the sheet so the straps fit you. Knot in place.

4.
When you've filled the pants with your hiking gear, tighten the belt to close the top of the satchel.

5.
You can decorate your satchel with puffy paint, embroidery or crests. It's also a great place to display all the buttons you've collected over the years.

HIKING ESSENTIALS

Check out the list below for the items you should take hiking, then turn to Day Hike (page 136) for how to plan a successful hike.

1. bandages
2. a thermos and cup
3. a garbage bag
4. tissues or toilet paper
5. sun screen
6. a hat
7. a raincoat
8. a notebook
9. a pencil
10. a yoghurt tub with holes in lid
11. insect repellent
12. a penknife
13. matches

TIN WHISTLE

A whistle can come in handy. You can use it to signal your friends, call your dog or take it on a hike to use if you get lost or separated from your friends. Here's how to make a simple whistle from a pop can.

You'll need:

1 aluminum can

a can opener

scissors or wire cutters

a pencil

an adult helper

1.
Ask an adult to help you cut off and discard the top of an aluminum can.

2.
Cut a 1-cm (½-inch) wide strip from the can. Flatten the strip and cut it into 2 pieces — 4 cm (1½ inches) long and 2 cm (¾ inch) long.

3.
Form a cross with the strips with 0.5 cm (¼ inch) extended at the top. Be careful of any sharp edges.

4.
Fold the ends of the shorter strip to the back. Don't pinch it tight. You need the air space for whistling.

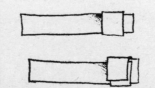

5.
Fold the top bit to the back.

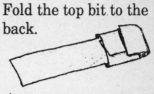

6.
Using a pencil, curl back the long end to form a little handle.

7.
Hold the whistle with your fingers covering the open "O" of the handle and blow.

DAY HIKE

Before you head out for a hike, you need a plan. You don't want to get lost, wander into a dangerous situation or get covered in poison ivy. Here's a formula for a safe and fun hike.

PLAN AHEAD

Your provincial department of natural resources sells very detailed local maps. You'll need one if you plan on a serious hike. A map will show you directions and point out cliffs, lakes, woods and marked trails on public property.

You can walk an average of 1.5 km (1 mile) in an hour. Plan stops for eating, exploring and lazing around. When you've decided your route, tell an adult where you're going and how long you think the hike will take.

It's fun to hike with a friend. You'll enjoy sharing the sights and sounds along the trail.

If you're hiking in the woods, don't forget to leave 1.5 m (5 feet) between you and your friend — you don't want a branch in the eye. Try to walk quietly, you'll see more wildlife.

WHAT TO TAKE

Turn to page 135 and see what to put in your expedition satchel or backpack. Don't forget a canteen of fresh water, a snack and a watch. You don't want to lug a heavy load, but there are a few essentials that will make sure you have a successful hike.

WHAT TO WEAR

Listen to the radio weather forecast first thing in the morning. Try to wear several light layers. It's better to take off extra clothes than to not have enough. Keep in mind sun, bugs, poison ivy and branches when you dress. A sun hat, cotton long-sleeved T-shirt, jeans, cotton socks and comfy running shoes are good hiking gear.

RULES OF THE TRAIL

1. Garbage on the trail can harm wildlife as well as spoil the natural beauty. Leave the trail a cleaner place. Pick up the trash of other less thoughtful hikers.
2. Respect private property. Always get permission before walking on private land or beaches.
3. Take photos or sketch plants and animal life instead of disturbing them.
4. Stick to the trails. Blazing your own path will damage plant life and you might get lost.
5. Be home before dark.

WATCH COMPASS

A watch can do more than tell you when to be home for dinner. If you become lost, you can use it to make a compass. Once you know where north is, you should be able to find your way home again.

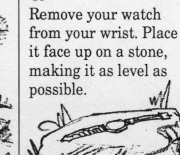

2.
Place a small twig on the edge of the watch face, opposite the hour hand. Move or rotate the watch until the stick's shadow lines up with the hour hand.

4.
This compass works only on sunny days. If it's cloudy, look for moss growing on tree trunks. It always grows on the north side of trees. Also, the sun always sets in the west. A well-planned hike will have you home for sunset!

1.
Remove your watch from your wrist. Place it face up on a stone, making it as level as possible.

3.
North is exactly half-way between the hour hand and 12. Always use the shortest way around the clock. For example, if it is 2 o'clock, north will point from 1 o'clock, not 7.

THE ITCHY PAGE

With the heat of summer come the bugs and plants that cause people to itch and scratch. Learning to identify the trouble makers could save you from some itchy situations.

POISON IVY

Poison ivy always has three pointed dark green leaves with jagged edges and slightly hairy undersides along with grey-white berries. Those seem to be the only features you can count on. Poison ivy likes to grow in shade but will grow in the sun, too. It can grow as a single, delicate plant or a woody vine that takes over a large area. Mostly the leaves are shiny, but they can be dull. However it appears, don't touch it.

The poisonous part of the plant is the oily sap. It can be spread by smoke from burning plants, on the fur of pets, from clothing or from touching the plant itself. If you think you've come in contact with poison ivy, wash your skin and clothes with soap and water right away.

You'll know you have a reaction to poison ivy if you develop a rash of tiny, intensely itchy, watery bumps. Ask a pharmacist for the best drug-store cure. Native Indians used the crushed stems of jewelweed rubbed on the rash. Jewelweed often grows alongside poison ivy and has yellow blooms that dangle down like earrings.

NETTLES

Even the name sounds prickly. Nettles, used by early settlers as a spinach-like food, are harmless when they first sprout. However, the mature plants have hairy spikes on the leaves and stems that can give you a nasty, stinging rash that feels like a burn. A pioneer cure for stinging nettles was to wash the rash with the sap from the dock plant. Watch out for nettles when you're exploring in marshy areas or along roadsides.

NETTLES

POISON IVY

MOSQUITOES

It's nearly impossible to escape mosquitoes. They are attracted to warmth, moisture, dark clothing and, worst of all, carbon dioxide. So, as long as you're breathing, a mosquito can find you. You can reduce the swarm buzzing for a bit by wearing light-coloured clothing that covers as much skin as possible. A carefully chosen repellent can ward off bugs, too. Why not try citronella? It's an all-natural oil made from citrus fruits. You can buy it in most drug stores.

When you're itchy, you scratch. But scratching doesn't stop the pain. Try to relieve the itch with a dab of lemon juice or rub with a peeled garlic clove. A paste made with baking soda and water helps take the itch out, too.

THE AMAZING MIDGE

Call them no-see-'ems, sand flies or midges. By any name, they give painful stings that cause very itchy, swollen welts. Like the mosquito, they are bloodsuckers, but they're so tiny, they can go right through clothing or a screen window to find a meal. Lucky for us, midges often feed on mosquitoes. Nice to know mosquitoes can be bitten, too!

Midges breed near water or in rotting vegetation. If you're swarmed by midges, the only thing to do is run — for the citronella.

BLACK FLIES

The May holiday weekend coincides with the hatching of black flies, or buffalo gnats. Black flies are less than 1 mm (1/8 inch) long, but their vicious bite can leave a bleeding and itchy crater on the skin. Like the mosquito, only the female bites in order to lay eggs. They live for three short weeks so they get right to work looking for a blood donor. They will attack livestock, wildlife, people and even other insects.

You can protect yourself from these blood hunters by wearing long-sleeved, long-legged clothing. They will attempt to climb under the clothing, so use an insect repellent around your wrists and ankles. Black flies are especially fond of tender areas, such as the back of your neck, so rub repellent on there, too, and wear a hooded jacket.

WILD SNACKS

WILD BERRY LEATHER ROLLS

Want your hike to be really on the wild side? Why not take along a few wild snacks for fun? Follow these safety rules, and your snacks will be nutritious, tasty and safe.

1. Use a field guide to identify plants and berries.
2. Never pick from the roadside where the plants may have been sprayed with chemicals.
3. Never pick an area clean — leave plants and berries to reproduce again.

You'll need:
500 mL (2 cups) wild strawberries or blackberries
a bowl
a potato masher
a platter
a piece of screening (optional)
a sprinkling of sugar
waxed paper
a jar

1.
Mash the berries to a pulp with the potato masher.

2.
Spread the mashed berries on a platter and lay them out to dry several days. Cover with the screening to keep away nibbling birds and insects.

(Ojibwa people used to lay the pulp on sheets of birchbark. You can do that, too, but don't pull the bark off a live tree. Use bark that has already fallen off.)

3.
When the pulp is dry, dust the leather with sugar.

4.
Roll up the leather like a jelly roll and cut it into easy-to-eat pieces.

5.
Carry the rolls in your backpack wrapped in waxed paper. Store extras in a clean, dry jar on the shelf.

WILD RASPBERRYADE

You'll need:

about 1 L (4 cups) wild raspberries

a large clean jar with a lid

250 mL (1 cup) vinegar (pioneers used cider vinegar)

2 clean J-cloths

2 saucepans

sugar

1.
Pack 500 mL (2 cups) of berries in the jar and pour in enough vinegar to cover them. Put on the lid and leave the jar in a cool place for 2 days.

2.
After 2 days, pour the berries into a J-cloth.

Squeeze the J-cloth full of berries so that the juice oozes out through the cloth and back into the jar. Discard the cloth and the strained berry pulp inside.

3.
Fill the jar again with the second 500 mL (2 cups) of fresh berries. Cover it and leave in a cool place for another 2 days.

4.
Squeeze and strain the pulp off again through another J-cloth and pour the juice into a saucepan.

5.
Pour 500 mL (2 cups) of sugar into a second saucepan and hold it

in one hand. Pick up the other saucepan with your other hand and compare the weights. Add or take away sugar until the two pans feel about the same weight.

6.
Add the sugar to the juice and boil for 10 minutes. Stir now and then.

7.
Chill the juice — this is a mix and must be kept covered in the fridge. To make raspberryade, add 30 to 45 mL (2 to 3 tbsp) of the mix to a glass of cold water or soda water. It makes a wild thirst-quencher for your hiking drink bottle.

Berries ripen in stages throughout the summer. Strawberries are ready in late June, raspberries by mid-July and blueberries ripen in August. Blackberries start about raspberry-time, but if you keep picking them, the bushes will produce well into August.

Unfortunately, there are poisonous berries out there, too. Never eat berries you're not sure about. Make certain you use a field guide or a knowledgeable adult to direct your berry-feasting!

BIRCHBARK BERRY BASKET

Use only bark that has fallen off a tree onto the ground, or from a dead tree. If you can't find any birchbark, there are directions for making your own on the next page.

You'll need:

1 piece of birchbark 25 cm x 30 cm (10 inches x 12 inches)
scissors
a ruler
a pencil
2 whittled sticks the size of toothpicks (or use toothpicks)

1.

If the birchbark is too stiff to bend, soak it for an hour in cool water.

2.

Trim the piece of birchbark to the correct size.

3.

With the ruler and pencil, draw 4 lines 7½ cm (3 inches) from the outside edges of the bark.

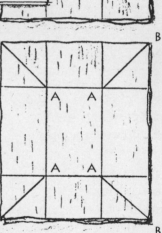

4.

The points where the lines intersect become points A and the corners become points B. Draw 4 lines from A to B as shown..

5.

Fold the bark and crease it along all the lines. To make the folds straight, line up the edges of the bark before making the fold.

6.

To form the berry basket, overlap the B folds at the ends.

7.

Using the sharp end of the scissor blades, pierce 2 holes in each end of the basket, through all thicknesses.

8.

Insert the sticks or toothpicks into one hole and out the other. Now all you need is a berry patch.

MOCK BARK

If you are unable to find birchbark on the ground, you can still make a berry basket using cardboard.

You'll need:
a piece of thin cardboard (with one white side if possible)
scissors
bark or corrugated cardboard
a black crayon

1.

A piece of cardboard from the packaging of new shirts or a file folder is about the same thickness as birchbark. Cut the cardboard to the correct size, 25 cm x 30 cm (10 inches x 12 inches).

2.

Place a piece of bark found from another tree, such as oak, or a piece of corrugated cardboard (the ripply kind found on the inside of boxes) under the cardboard.

3.

Using the black crayon, rub lightly on the white side of the cardboard. The lines you make will look like birchbark. Use your mock bark to make a berry basket by following the instructions in Birchbark Berry Basket.

COOKOUT

Smoke in your eyes, yummy smells in your nose and crackling fire sounds in your ears. That's right, it's time for a cookout. Everything tastes wonderful when you're the chef. All you need is a roasting stick, an open fire and some food. (See page 114 for choosing a safe fire site and building a small fire.) Here are some really scrumptious ideas for your cookouts this summer.

SMORES

You'll need:
marshmallows
a bar of chocolate
graham wafers

Squishy and sweet, smores are an easy cookout dessert.

1.
Roast your marshmallow until golden brown.

2.
Make a gooey sandwich of marshmallow and chocolate between two graham crackers.

3.
Don't forget to lick your fingers before you say, "I want smore, please!"

BREAKFAST BAKE

You'll need:
a knife
an orange
an egg
a fork

1.
Cut the orange in half and eat it.

2.
Pull out all the membranes to form a perfect orange-rind coddling cup.

3.
Have someone hold the cup while you crack the egg into it.

4.
Use two sticks to gently lower the cup into the coals of a low fire. Cook for approximately 5 minutes. Eat the egg right from the rind.

HOLE POTATO

Potatoes can be baked whole, in a hole.

You'll need:
- a potato
- a penknife
- butter (optional)
- salt and pepper (optional)

1. Before you light your fire, scoop out a small pit in the ground.

2. Wash the potato and poke it several times with your penknife before tossing the potato in the small pit.

3. Cover the potato with ashes from a previous fire.

4. Build your fire on top of your buried potato. Your hole potato will take about an hour to cook.

5. Let the fire die down before retrieving your potato with the help of a roasting stick.

6. Cut the potato open and add butter, salt and pepper. Corn on the cob can be cooked with this method, too. Just leave the corn in its husk and bake as the potato.

BANNOCK

Bannock, or wilderness bread, is flat and chewy and tastes great with butter and jam.

You'll need:
- 250 mL (1 cup) of flour
- a big pinch of salt
- 10 mL (2 tsp) of baking powder
- a bowl
- a fork
- 15 mL (1 tbsp) of margarine
- slightly less than 125 mL (½ cup) of milk
- a frying pan

1. Combine all the dry ingredients in the bowl.

2. Use a fork to stir in the margarine and milk. Stir until most of the lumps are out.

3. With floured fingers, make a 3-cm (1-inch) thick loaf.

4. Push the dough into an ungreased frying pan. Bake over a low fire for 7 or 8 minutes on each side, turning with a stick.

5. Eat your bannock warm as it comes or with butter, jam or peanut butter.

145

SLEEP-OUT

If you've tried a day hike, a few cookouts and you're feeling outdoor smart, how about learning some real wilderness skills? Like building a lean-to, starting a fire with no matches and weaving a comfortable bed — all from found materials.

On the next pages, you'll find the directions to teach yourself these skills. The directions assume you've got some of the essentials all good campers have — food, water, a good knife, a hatchet and rope.

NATURAL ROPE OR STRING

If you forget to take rope along, it's easy to make your own. Look for a dead cedar tree, cut off the outer bark and then peel long strips of the inner bark still stuck to the wood. You can braid the strips or twist several together to make rope. A piece of rope can be lengthened by tying some of the strips over a bough, twisting them together, then twisting more strips into the end over and over until you've got the length you need.

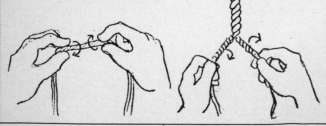

CONSTRUCTING A LEAN-TO

Check out the area for materials you can use for a lean-to. Depending on the site, there may be natural features you can use that'll cut down on your preparation and work. Standing trees that are the right distance apart, for instance, can be used instead of cutting and erecting end poles.

You'll need:
a supply of poles, including a long ridge pole and 2 sturdy end poles — use only dead wood
rope
a supply of moss, boughs and handfuls of dead, lichen-covered branches

1.
Site your lean-to in a sheltered spot so that the prevailing wind blows across the front opening. (See page 161, to find out how to tell wind direction.)

2.
Strip the poles of branches with your knife or hatchet. Remember to direct your knife strokes away from your body (see Knife Safety on page 117).

3.
A lean-to starts out as a skeleton of poles looking a bit like a hockey net. The ridge or crossbar pole can be lashed between two trees and propped up at each end by smaller poles wedging it in place.

The ridge pole has to be high enough so more poles, leaning down the back, can be laid at a steep angle and still leave enough room underneath for a person to sit. The steeper the angle, the more waterproof the lean-to. The front of the lean-to is open, but the two sides should also be banked with poles.

4.

Once the skeleton is standing securely, stuff and chink between the poles with moss and then tie on dead boughs (stem up, underside facing out) to a depth of 30 cm (12 inches) thick. Even better than boughs are handfuls of dead, lichen-covered branches held in place by a second row of leaning poles. Don't forget to pack the two ends as well as the back of the lean-to.

SITING
THE CAMPFIRE

Even in a real survival situation, don't consider a campfire in front of the lean-to unless you've sited it so the opening is lengthwise to the wind. In other words, the wind blows into one of the two sides of the lean-to. If the open mouth of the lean-to faces the wind, sparks and smoke will choke your living space. If the back of the lean-to faces the wind, air rising over it will create backdrafts with the heat of the fire, and smoke will be a problem again.

WIND

If the lean-to is sited correctly (so the prevailing wind blows across the opening), you can put a small campfire several long steps in front of it. The smoke and any sparks will drift past the opening, and even a backdraft won't take the fire or smoke dangerously over your shelter. A campfire cooks food with the heat rising up with the smoke, but it warms you with the radiant heat that glows out the sides. Sited correctly, radiant heat from the fire will glow into your lean-to and give you a gentle warmth.

BEDDING DOWN

Here's how to make a comfy mattress and bed frame for a campout in the wild — or for lolling on beside the cottage while you're reading a great book.

In making this mattress, you construct a simple but huge weaving loom that actually turns into the supporting bed frame when you're finished.

You'll need:
an adult helper
a hammer
2 strong nails at least 4 cm (1½ inches) long
a sledge hammer or good rock for pounding
8 1-m (3-foot) wooden sticks about 3 cm (1 inch) thick
a hatchet
30 m (100 feet) of strong cord cut into 5-m (16-foot) lengths
a good supply of bulrushes or reeds (even hay will do)
about 3 m (10 feet) of sturdy string

1.

Find two trees about a metre (3 feet) apart. Nail and lash one of the sticks between the trees to form a fixed crossbar, just less than a metre (3 feet) above the ground.

2.

Select 6 of the remaining sticks and sharpen one end of each with the hatchet so they can be easily driven into the ground. Always chop or stroke with the blade directed away from you.

3.

Pound the 6 stakes part way into the ground, 2 m (7 feet) in front of the fixed crossbar and about 15 cm (6 inches) apart.

4.

Lay the last stick on the ground, behind the stakes and 3 m (10 feet) in front of the fixed crossbar, but parallel to it. This will become the free, moving crossbar of your loom.

5.

Tie one 5-m (16-foot) length of cord to an outside stake, loop it tightly around the fixed crossbar between the trees and pull it back to tie on the end of the free crossbar.

Repeat this with each length of cord and each stake. Try to keep the cords equal distances apart on the fixed crossbar and the tension the same between the crossbars. When you've finished, you'll have 6 stationary cords running from the stakes pounded into the ground to the fixed crossbar. You'll also have 6 loose cords wrapped around the fixed crossbar and returning past the stakes and tied in 6 knots along the free crossbar. When you lift the free crossbar up, the loose cords attached to it come, too, but the cords that run between the fixed crossbar and the stakes lie stationary.

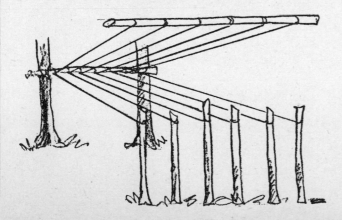

6.

Now it's time to weave. Raise the free crossbar up into the air to separate the loose and stationary cords and place a bunch of rushes between them. Push the rushes evenly and tightly against the fixed crossbar.

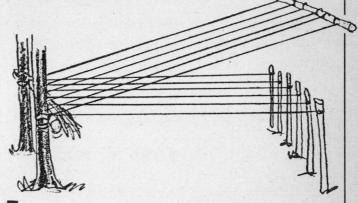

7.

Drop the free crossbar to the ground and lay another bunch of rushes between the cords. Squish them up against those already woven in.

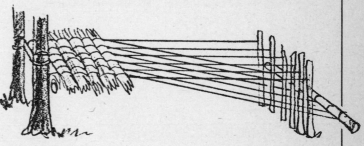

8.

Continue weaving in rushes by repeating steps 6 and 7 until the full length of the mattress is made.

9.

Lash the free crossbar to the row of stakes with sturdy string to complete the bed frame and add extra support. Now, lie back and enjoy the comfort of your hand-made bed.

MATCHLESS FIRE

Imagine that you're alone in the wilderness as night falls. It's cold and drizzling rain. You reach for your pack of matches to start a warm and friendly fire. Oh no! — they're soaking wet. What can you do?

You can light a fire without matches or paper. All you need is a spark and lots of tinder to catch fire. Practise the skill at your next family fire pit. Then you'll know what to do in an emergency.

FINDING THE BEST TINDER

Tinder can be the inner bark of dead trees, twigs shredded between your fingers, dead grass — anything that will flash into fire from just a spark. The best tinder is very dry, shredded into small pieces and loosely packed so it will not fall apart.

If you are near a meadow, look for an abandoned bird or mouse nest in the long grass. The dried-out straw makes terrific tinder.

So does silk from milkweed pods, cattail fluff and abandoned wasps' nests.

In an evergreen forest, look for brown, dried-up twigs on the lower branches of spruce, balsam or cedar trees.

Even in heavy rain, you'll find dry dead twigs and bark low down on the tree trunks.

In a deciduous forest, look for coils of wispy birchbark on the ground. Birchbark is good tinder even when it's damp.

When you have enough tinder to form a small nest, find a sheltered spot to lay your fire. (Check page 114 for tips on setting a campfire safely.) Collect dry branches for kindling and pile them nearby so that once you have a flame, you can start feeding it.

MAKING THE **SPARK**

Now it's time for a spark to set that tinder ablaze. You can make a spark by striking flint and steel together. You can't use just any rocks, you have to have special kinds, but they aren't hard to find. First, look for a glassy stone — quartz, agate, jasper or flint will all do fine. Choose a broken piece with a sharp edge. Then, find a hunk of iron pyrites — you probably know it as fool's gold.

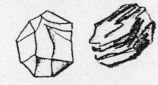

If iron pyrites isn't common in your area, anything made of steel will do. Use a pocket knife, nail file or other small utensil made of steel.

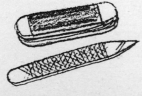

Curl your tinder loosely into a nest in the centre of the campfire ring. Strike the sharp edge of the stone with steel until sparks fall down into the tinder nest. If you're having trouble getting a spark, try to keep your striking wrist as loose as possible.

When the tinder catches the spark, you'll see a puff of smoke.

Then you must cup your hands around the nest and blow in quick, gentle puffs until you see a flame.

Slowly start adding small pieces of kindling (see page 116) to build up a cosy, warm fire.

WATERPROOF MATCHES

Instead of finding yourself with no easy way to make a fire when you need it, plan ahead. Carry waterproofed matches and a strip of sandpaper. Always carry matches in a plastic bag.

You can waterproof matches yourself. Take about ten wooden matches and hold them in a bundle. Dip them, tips and all, into melted wax.

After the wax hardens, put them in a bag. When it's time to start a fire, separate off one match, peel the wax off its tip with your fingernail and strike it on the sandpaper.

RAINY DAYS

Your summer day can be fun even if it's windy, cool or raining. In fact, this section will help you forecast rotten days ahead of time. Relax inside and make a fun mask or a knotted bracelet. Why not try origami or construct a beading loom? The activities on the following pages can make the best summer days out of the worst rainy days.

WEATHER WIZARD

Amaze yourself and your friends by predicting tomorrow's weather today. Just make the simple instruments in Sunny Highs (below) and Sunny Drys (page 156), and you can use them to forecast sun or rain.

SUNNY HIGHS

When air pressure is rising, good weather can be expected. When air pressure starts to fall, poor weather may be on the way. You can tell when air pressure is rising or falling by checking a barometer. Here's an easy way you can make your own barometer.

You'll need:
Plasticine or other modelling clay
a flat-bottomed bowl
a ruler
a tall, narrow, clear plastic bottle
string
paper
pencil
sticky tape

1.
Stick a hunk of Plasticine towards one side of the bottom of your bowl and use it to hold the ruler upright.

2.
Fill both the plastic bottle and the bowl three-quarters full with water.

3.
Cover the mouth of the bottle with one hand, turn it upside-down with the other and carefully lower the bottle into the bowl. When the bottle mouth is underwater, you can pull away your wet hand, but be sure to keep the bottle steady until it's balanced on the bottom and supported by the ruler.

4.

Tie the bottle to the ruler with string in at least two places.

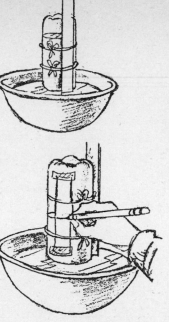

5.

Slip a strip of paper under the string so it sits up and down on the face of the bottle. Tape it there. With your pencil, mark a line on the paper to show the present water level inside the bottle.

6.

Look to see if the water level has changed each day from the day before. At the beginning of a clear, dry day, you'll find the water level inside the bottle has moved high up the stick. Mark the level of that "high" on your strip of paper. At the onset of stormy, wet weather, the water level inside the bottle will have fallen low. Mark the level of that "low" on the paper.

7.

Store your barometer in a cool place, away from the sun so that the water in it will not evaporate.

8.

When you want to forecast the weather, check to see if your barometer is rising or falling. Do this by noting the water level and then coming back in a while and looking again. Expect good weather when the water level in the bottle is creeping towards "high," rainy weather when the water level is dipping "low" and unsettled, windy weather when the level is changing rapidly.

HOW DOES IT WORK?

Even though we don't feel it, air in the atmosphere presses down on the Earth all the time. Sometimes that pressure is a little stronger than other times. In your barometer, the air presses down on the water in the bowl. When the air pressure is high, it pushes so hard that some of the water is pushed right up into the bottle, raising the water level in the bottle.  When the air pressure is low, the opposite happens and the water in the bottle lowers. High pressure brings good weather, low pressure brings poor weather. Air pressure starts to change before the weather does, so a barometer forecasts what's coming by detecting those changes early.

✱✱✱✱✱✱✱✱✱✱✱✱✱✱✱✱✱✱✱✱✱✱✱✱

SUNNY DRYS

You can usually count on good weather when the air is dry. As moisture or humidity in the air builds, so does the chance of rain. You can measure humidity by using this hygrometer you make yourself.

You'll need:
scissors
a 20-cm (8-inch) strip of coloured, lightweight cardboard
tacks
a block of wood at least 20 cm x 4 cm (8 inches x 1½ inches)
a square of heavy cardboard at least 20 cm x 20 cm (8 inches x 8 inches)
sticky tape
a human hair about 20 cm (8 inches) long
a marker pen

1.

Cut an arrow from the strip of lightweight cardboard as shown.

2.

Tack the wood block behind the stiff cardboard square to hold it standing upright.

3.

Tape one end of the hair at the top of the upright board.

4.

Hold your arrow across the face of the board so the pointer sits right over the loose end of the hair. Stab a tack through the blunt end of the arrow and on through the board. (You may want to form a tiny ball of eraser or chewing gum on the sharp end of the tack so that it won't fall out.)

5.

Tape the loose end of hair to the back of the head of the arrow.

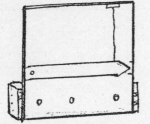

6.

On a dry, sunny day, mark where the arrow rests on the board with the word "dry." On a rainy day, mark where the arrow rests with the word "humid."

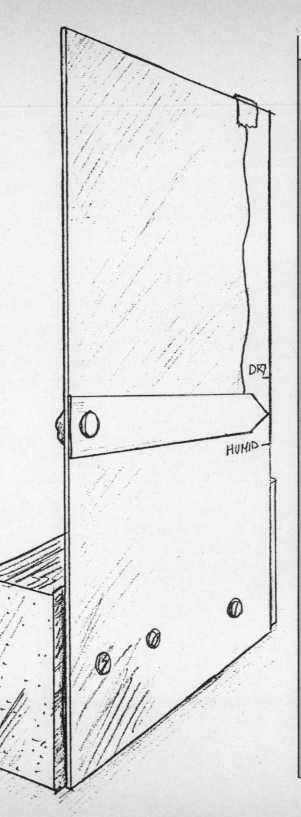

DRY

HUMID

HOW DOES IT WORK?

Because human hair lengthens with moisture and shrinks with dryness, your arrow will drop a little if the air is humid and rise if it's dry. If your arrow drops to "humid" and the day is hot, watch for a thunderstorm. If your arrow rises to dry, you can put away your raincoat for a while.

NATURAL WEATHER REPORTS

Did you know dandelions forecast the weather? On sunny days, the dandelion flower is open. But before it rains, the dandelion closes tightly so that none of its precious pollen gets wet. How does the plant know?

Dandelions have an amazing sensitivity to moisture that you can test. Pick a dandelion stalk, make a few slits in the bottom of the stem and then put it in water. Before long, the ends of the stem will curl up. Meanwhile, the dandelion flower head reacts in the same way and pulls up tightly when it senses moisture.

Like dandelions, most wildlife seem to know when good weather or bad is coming. By watching and listening to plants and animals, you can learn to predict the weather, too.

Watch for some of the plant and animal behaviours on this page so you can forecast rain or shine.

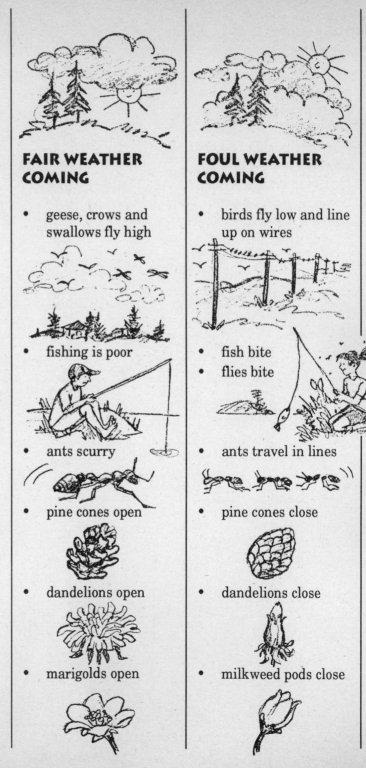

FAIR WEATHER COMING

- geese, crows and swallows fly high

- fishing is poor

- ants scurry

- pine cones open

- dandelions open

- marigolds open

FOUL WEATHER COMING

- birds fly low and line up on wires

- fish bite
- flies bite

- ants travel in lines

- pine cones close

- dandelions close

- milkweed pods close

WILDLIFE AND THUNDERSTORMS

Watch how the natural world reacts to an approaching summer thunderstorm and you'll know how long you've got to take cover. If you first notice the storm when the sky begins to darken, think about it. You've probably been aware of little changes for at least an hour. You may have noticed that everything smells more strongly — even lake water smells before a storm. If you're near a campfire, the smoke may have been bothering your eyes — another sign of poor weather on the way.

The storm is still a few minutes off if birds are noisy, active and restless and if insects are busy biting. But when the birds suddenly disappear and all is strangely quiet, take immediate shelter or you'll get soaked.

CRICKETS CHIRP OUT THE HEAT

The hotter the day, the more often a cricket chirps. You can actually tell the temperature by counting the number of chirps you hear. All you need is a watch and a chirping cricket. Here's what to do:

1.

Count the number of cricket chirps you hear in 15 seconds.

2.

Divide this number by 2 and add 6. Your answer is the temperature in degrees Celsius. (To get a reading in Fahrenheit, simply add 40 to the number of chirps in 15 seconds.)

Suppose it's hot outside, and you hear 40 chirps in 15 seconds.

40 divided by 2 is 20

20 add 6 is 26

The temperature is 26°C.
(Or, 40 plus 40 is 80°F.)

Now that's heat with a beat!

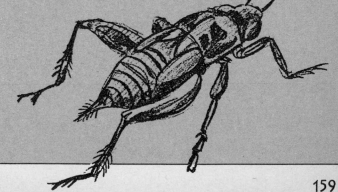

WEATHER PROOFS

If you use some of the methods on the last few pages, your weather forecasting should be right on most of the time, but there will be days you'll be fooled.

You can set up a weather recording system and track the true weather. Keep records of temperature, rainfall and wind on a calendar so you can compare statistics day to day.

TEMPERATURE

Whether you use a cricket thermometer (see page 159) or a thermometer on the wall, record the temperature at about 1:00 p.m. to determine the daily high. (The daily low is usually at 3 a.m., when most people are asleep.) Write down the daily high on your calendar, and at the end of your holiday you'll be able to tell which day was the hottest.

RAINFALL

A narrow, sturdy tin sitting in an open area will collect daily rainfall. After a shower or storm, take a ruler to your cup, measure the number of millimetres that fell and record that number on your calendar. Do it right after the rain stops and before any evaporates away. If the amount collected is so small you can't measure it, use "T" for "trace" on your calendar.

160

WIND

About 200 years ago an Englishman named Admiral Beaufort worked out a scale to measure wind force by noting the effect of wind on trees. You can use the Beaufort Scale to record the wind force.

Force 0
Calm. Leaves, branches, trees stand still.

Force 1-3
Light breeze. Leaves and small branches move.

Force 4-5
Moderate wind. Small trees sway.

Force 6-7
Strong wind. Big trees sway.

Force 8-9
Gale. Leaves and twigs snap off trees.

Force 10-11
Storm. Large branches break off trees, widespread damage.

Force 12
Hurricane or tornado. Large trees fall down, disaster.

Wind statistics usually include wind direction as well as its force. Once you know where north, south, east and west are, find a flag or a bending tree and then decide from which direction the wind is blowing. A flag or tree blowing towards the south is pushed there by a wind driving from the north, and you call that a north wind.

If you don't have a flag to look at, you can figure out wind direction with nothing more than your own body. Suck the end of one finger and hold it up high. The side that feels coolest will face the direction the wind is blowing.

WEATHER ROCK

If you prefer things to be simple, there's always the weather rock. A weather rock is any rock you place out in the open. If the rock is wet, the weather is wet. If the rock is cold, the temperature is cold. If the rock is warm, the temperature is warm. If the rock is buried in snow, it's been snowing. If the rock is blowing away — watch out!

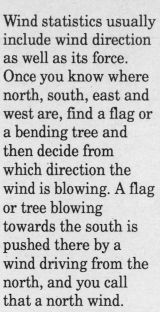

FAN-TASTIC

What's your favourite way to beat the heat? Jump in the lake or take a breezy bike ride? Read the hot-weather tips on this page then make this fan on a rainy day so you'll be ready to fan away the heat when the sun shines again.

Dress in lightweight and light-coloured clothing, drink lots of water and don't over-exercise between 11:00 a.m. and 2:00 p.m., the hottest time of day. Animals feel the heat, too. Don't  forget your cat or dog also needs fresh water to drink.

Wildlife have their own ways of cooling down. When polar bears find the summer months too warm, they dig down into the permafrost, where it is always frozen, and curl up in an icy bed. Hippos spend the heat of the day submerged in a river, with nothing but their nostrils sticking out. Many kinds of animals cool off with a swim, including bears, moose, wolves, birds and even lions. Fish dive to deeper and colder water. Animals also know to take a nap when it's really hot. From cats and dogs to chipmunks and sea gulls, the animal world lazes around from noon till four. One way you can beat the heat is to make a cooling fan.

You'll need:
a hammer
a small sharp nail
7 sticks the size of Popsicle sticks
a twist tie
newspaper
scissors
heavy construction paper
felt tip markers
white glue

1.
Using the hammer and nail, make a small hole in the end of each stick.

2.
Pull the twist tie through the holes of all 7 sticks. Make a neat loop with the twist tie and twist it to secure the sticks together.

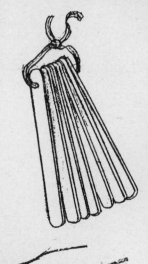

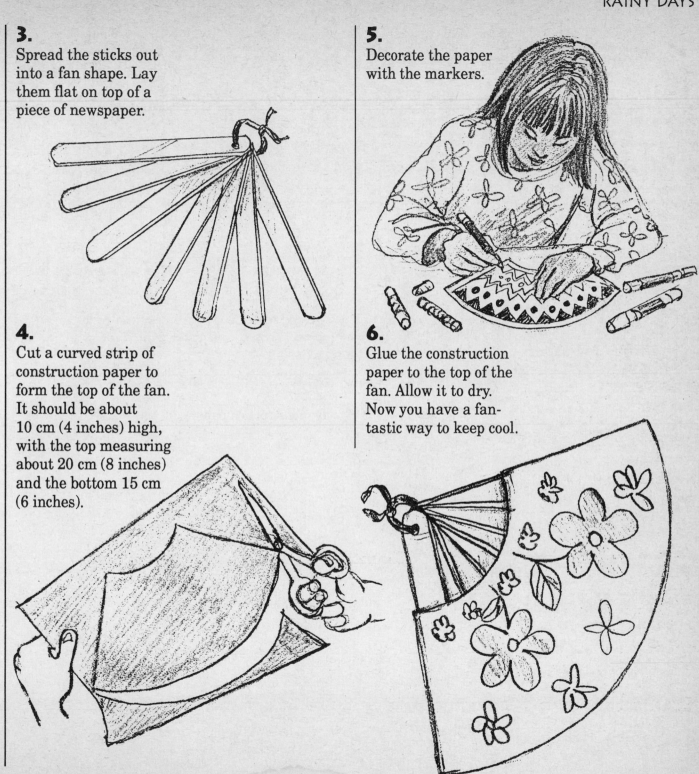

3.
Spread the sticks out into a fan shape. Lay them flat on top of a piece of newspaper.

4.
Cut a curved strip of construction paper to form the top of the fan. It should be about 10 cm (4 inches) high, with the top measuring about 20 cm (8 inches) and the bottom 15 cm (6 inches).

5.
Decorate the paper with the markers.

6.
Glue the construction paper to the top of the fan. Allow it to dry. Now you have a fantastic way to keep cool.

RAINY-DAY GAMES

Brighten up those dull, rainy days at the cottage with a boxful of games you've made yourself.

SHOWERY SHUFFLEBOARD

You'll need:

a ruler

a pencil

a piece of cardboard
60 x 80 cm
(24 inches x 32 inches)

4 pennies

1.
Using your ruler, draw a triangle with one point in the middle of the cardboard. Divide the triangle up into sections with points ranging from 5 to 15 as shown. Make two -1 sections for when you miss getting on target.

2.
Draw a line 5 cm (2 inches) from the opposite end of the board. You can't move your hand over this line when taking a shot.

3.
With a friend, choose heads or tails and take two pennies each.
Heads goes first.

4.
Place the game board on a table or floor. Slide the penny back and forth and then release it at the line, aiming for the triangle. Tails takes a turn, also aiming for the triangle. Keep taking turns until someone scores 100 points. (Hint: Try to knock your opponent's pennies out of the triangle. If you knock any into the -1 section, she loses a point.)

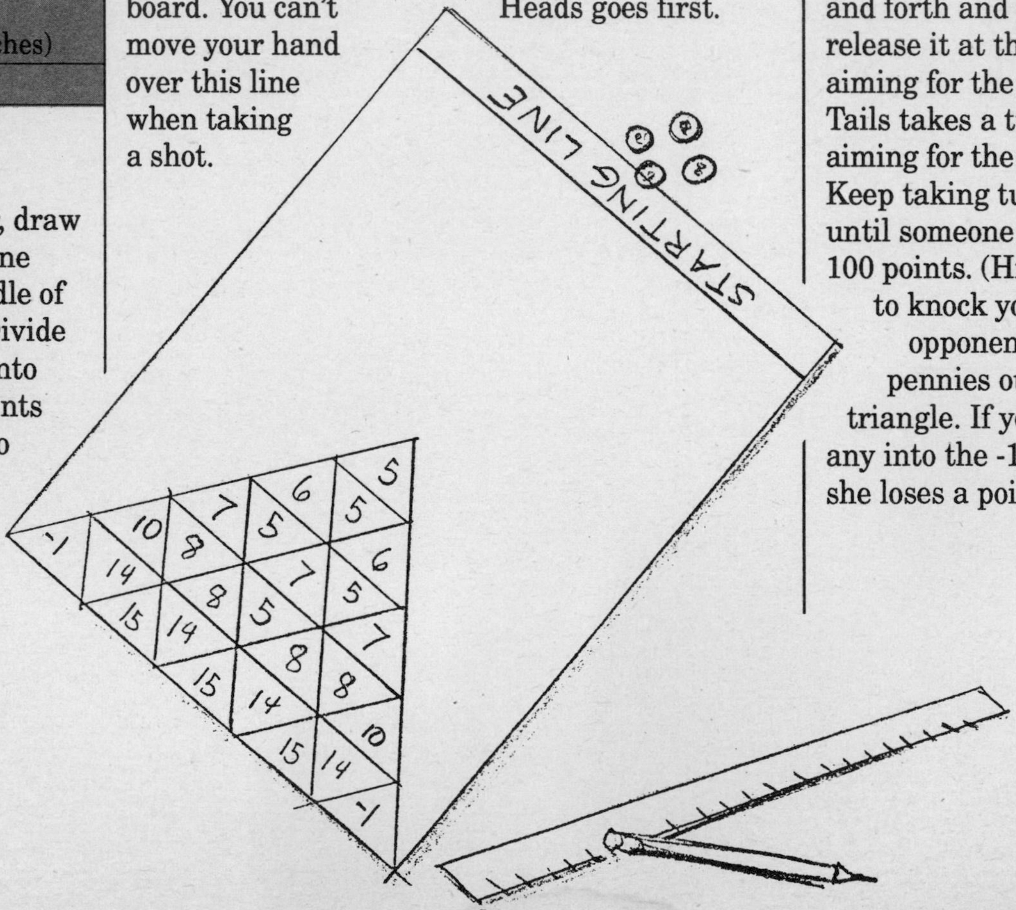

THUNDERSTORM TRAY GAME

You'll need:

25 small objects from around the cottage

a tray

a tea towel

pencils

paper

1.
Collect small objects from all over the cottage — cotter pins, soap dish, nail brush, tweezers, nail, bird feather, salt shaker, spool of thread — anything you find that will fit on the tray.

2.
Place them on the tray and cover it with a tea towel.

3.
Challenge everyone to see how many things they can remember after having only 25 seconds to look at the tray. Let them write them down. Whoever remembers the most items wins.

4.
Ask them to challenge you with a different assortment or have them remove some of your objects and see if you can quickly guess what's missing.

SOLITARY HOURS

You'll need:

1 deck of cards

1.
Shuffle the deck well. Set up the game by making a clock shape. Starting at 1 o'clock, lay down one card at a time in a clockwise direction — 1, 2, 3, 4, etc., up to 12. Place a card in the middle. Continue to lay down from 1 through 13 until all 13 piles have four cards.

2.
Starting in the middle, pick the top card. If this is a 3, place it on top of 3 o'clock and take the next card from the top of the 3 pile. Jacks are 11, queens are 12 and kings are 13.

3.
Continue until all 4 kings appear in the middle. Then it is time to redeal.

PAPER FOLDING

By learning the traditional Japanese art of paper folding or origami, you can turn a scrap of paper into a leaping frog, an elegant swan or a delicate boat.

If you like origami, borrow a book on the art of paper folding from the local library and try more complicated figures. The instructions on these pages will give you some of the basics you'll need to go on creating origami art.

You'll need:
scissors
paper — uncrumpled and crisp is best, but newspaper will do
a ruler

1.

For folding a frog, cut paper 6 cm x 10 cm (2½ inches x 4 inches). For making a swan, cut paper 15 cm x 15 cm (6 inches x 6 inches). For a boat, use a regular-sized piece of letter paper — 20 cm x 27 cm (8½ inches x 11 inches). Trim the edges so the measurements are exact on all sides and the angles are square.

frog
6 cm x 10 cm
(2½ inches x
4 inches)

swan
15 cm x 15 cm
(6 inches x
6 inches)

boat
20 cm x 27 cm
(8½ inches x
11 inches)

2.

Follow the diagram instructions using this symbol key:

valley fold (the valley fold points away from you)

mountain fold (the mountain fold forms a ridge pointing towards you)

crease (a crease is a line on the paper made by making a fold and then opening it up flat again)

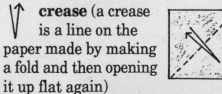

turn over (turn the paper over before making the next fold)

3.
Fold, crease and turn the paper as the diagrams direct, working in the order indicated by the numbers. Remember to set up each fold carefully, with corners matching and edges meeting. Rub a fingernail along every fold, so the line is clean and sharp.

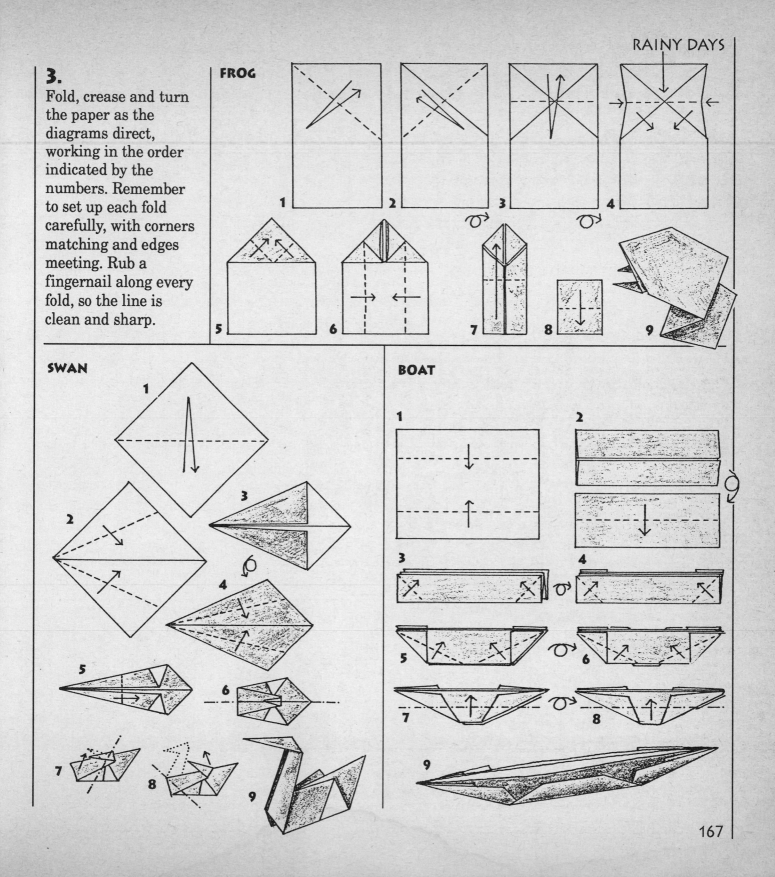

FROG

SWAN

BOAT

167

BEADING LOOM

Beading is a North American handicraft that is fun to do, especially if you make your own loom. You can make bracelets, anklets, headbands and bookmarks or decorate belts and backpacks.

You'll need:

a hand saw

a fine-toothed comb 12 cm (5 inches) long

a hammer and nail

sandpaper

2 pieces of wood 10 cm x 7 cm (4 inches x 3 inches)

a screwdriver

14 wood screws

wood glue

2 pieces of wood 35 cm x 2 cm (14 inches x $^3/_4$ inch)

1 piece of wood 35 cm x 7 cm (14 inches x 3 inches)

white polyester thread, or elastic thread for bracelets and rings

tiny beads

a beading needle (very skinny)

1.
Carefully saw the comb in half. Use the hammer and nail to make holes in the plastic handles 1 cm ($^1/_2$ inch) in from each side of the two combs.

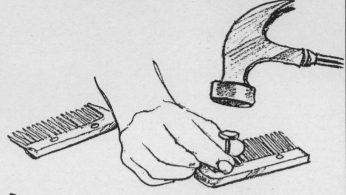

2.
Sand all the pieces of wood until they are smooth.

3.
Attach the combs to the small end pieces of wood by placing the handle of each comb 1 cm ($^1/_2$ inch) below the top of the end piece, leaving the teeth of the comb protruding above the wood. Screw through the holes in the plastic handle, into the wood.

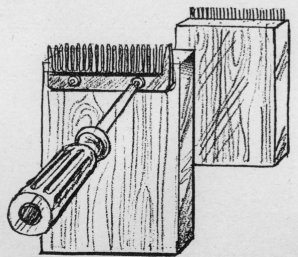

4.
Glue the 2 pieces of wood 35 cm x 2 cm (14 inches x ³/₄ inch) to the edges of the larger piece, 35 cm x 7 cm (14 inches x 3 inches). Allow them to dry. This creates a little well in the middle of the loom to catch fallen beads.

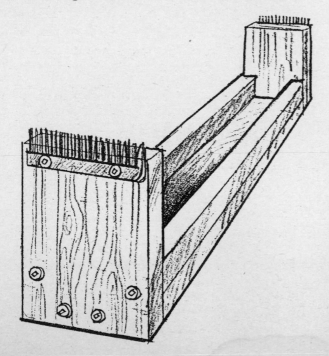

5.
Attach the end pieces to the glued pieces of wood, using four screws on each end as shown.

6.
To secure the threads, you will need one screw positioned in the middle of each end, 2 cm (³/₄ inch) up from the bottom, below the combs. Screw half-way into the wood.

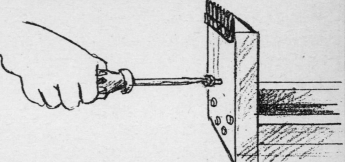

7.
To thread the loom for a bookmark 3 cm (1 inch) wide, you'll need to cut 11 pieces of thread, 50 cm (20 inches) long.

8.
Wind each thread around one screw, through the teeth of one comb across the loom, through the other comb and around the other screw. Proceed until you have threaded across 3 cm (1 inch) of the comb. Turn the page to find out how to start beading.

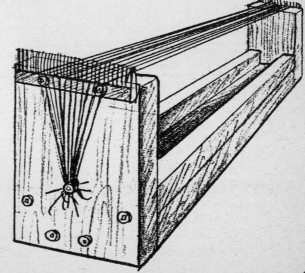

BEADING

Once you've set up your loom (see page 168), you are ready to begin your first beading project. Choose the beads you want to use and place them in a small, heavy bowl.

1.

Thread the beading needle with about 1 m (3 feet) of thread. If the eye of the needle is too small for the thread, stretch it wider using a pin or another needle. Do not double or knot the thread.

2.

Place the loom between your legs, with one comb at your knees and the other near your stomach.

3.

Knot the beading thread to the outside left-hand thread of the loom.

4.

Pull 10 beads through the needle and onto the beading thread.

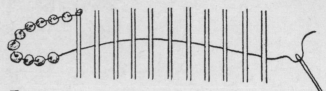

5.

Place the needle underneath the loom threads. Use your finger to position each bead between two loom threads.

6.

Draw the needle through the bead holes from right to left, above the loom threads.

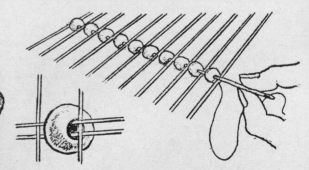

7.

Keep the beading thread taut. The row of beads should lie flat between the loom threads.

8.

Continue to weave beads exactly as you did in the first row.

9.

To change needle thread, weave the end piece of your first thread back into the previous rows, and remove the needle. Cut a new piece of thread, rethread the needle and run the needle through several rows of beads. Knot the second thread around the outside loom thread and continue where you left off. Keep beading until your bookmark is the length of a paperback book.

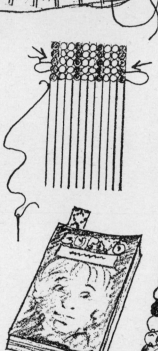

BEADING DESIGNS

Once you have the hang of beading on a loom, you'll want to create your own designs. Use graph paper and coloured pencils to sketch out your designs. Your own personalized bookmark is easy to do. Highlight your name in one colour and make the background another colour.

FINISHING OFF

When you've finished your project, you must tie off the threads to prevent the beads from unravelling.

1.

To make a fringe, remove the threads from the screw at one end. Start at the outside edge and thread the first loom thread with the beading needle. Pass the needle through 8 beads, then, bypassing the eighth bead, loop back through the other 7 beads. Weave in the excess thread and trim. Thread the next loom thread and reinforce the fringe by going down through the 8 beads and reversing back through 7. Repeat this for all the loom threads.

2.

To make a straight edge, simply weave the remaining bead thread back through your work. Untie the loom threads from the screw and work each one back into the beading. Now you may sew your design onto your backpack, hat or belt.

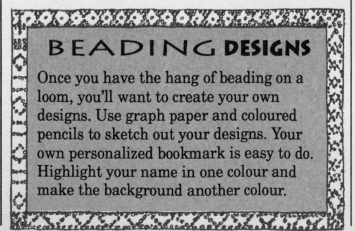

171

KNOTTING BRACELETS

With a safety pin and colourful embroidery thread, you can spend a lazy afternoon making an easy, fun-to-wear bracelet.

You'll need:

scissors

3 colours of embroidery thread

a safety pin

1.
Cut 6 strands of embroidery thread, 2 of each colour and about an arm's length each.

2.
Put the ends of the threads together and tie them in a knot to the safety pin.

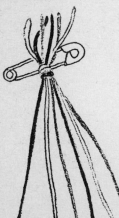

3.
Attach the safety pin to the knee of your jeans or a pillow. Pull the strands of thread towards you and adjust the knot so the threads lie flat on your lap.

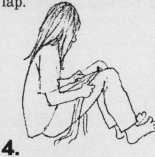

4.
In your mind, label the left thread 1, the thread to its immediate right 2, then 3 and so on to 6.

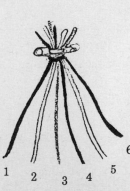

5.
Hold 1 in your right hand.

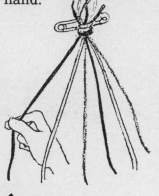

6.
Put your left hand under 2 and pull it down with your four fingers. At the same time, stick up your left thumb so it juts between threads 1 and 2.

7.
With your right hand, pick up 1, pull it in front of your left thumb and across 2. You should be looking down at a right-angled triangle or "L" shape made from thread 1 crossing 2.

8.
With 1 still crossing over the top of 2, slip it around and under 2, and then up into the centre of the triangle. Pull 1, releasing your left thumb as you tighten the knot towards the safety pin.

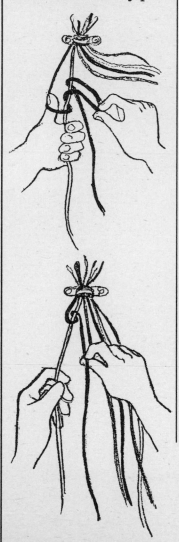

9.
Make a second knot on top of the first with threads 1 and 2. It always takes 2 knots to make a stitch.

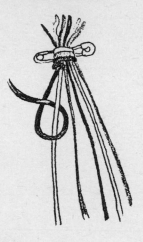

10.
Now, lay thread 2 off to the left, pull 1 straight down and grab thread 3 with the four fingers of your left hand. Stick up your left thumb so it juts between 1 and 3. There is a front and a back to your bracelet, so don't let your work flip over — always work on the same side.

11.
Repeat steps 5 to 7, and then move on so you are working with 1 and 4.

12.
Continue until you've worked thread 1 across all the others and then straighten out the results. Thread 2 should be at the left-most side now. Treat it as 1 and repeat steps 4 to 9.

13.
Continue to work the pattern until the bracelet just fits around your wrist. Get a friend to tie it on and leave it on all summer. A knotted bracelet will keep looking great — swim after swim.

14.
After some practice, try creating different effects by using some threads of the same colour or by increasing to 9 strands across.

MASK MAKING

You can make a mask out of a paper plate, a paper bag or an old pair of sunglasses, but a mask that is moulded to the true shape of your own face is much more interesting. Here's an easy way to make a face-fitting mask so you can give yourself a fantastical look.

You'll need:
scissors
kraft paper or paper torn from heavy brown grocery bags
a mirror
a toothpick
white glue
newspaper
watercolour paints
a paintbrush
seeds, feathers, pebbles, dried mushrooms, string, bottle caps, stamps, pine needles, pasta pieces and other found materials for decoration

1.
Cut a strip of kraft paper about 1 cm (½ inch) wide and long enough to make a headband across your forehead and around the back of your head. Look into the mirror, and using the toothpick as a gluestick, glue it to fit. Be careful not to get glue on your face or hair.

2.
Cut 3 more strips of 1-cm (½-inch) wide paper. Look in the mirror, fit and glue one strip to circle from the headband in front of one ear, around the front of your chin and up to the headband in front of your other ear. Arrange the other 2 strips to form a cross on top of your head, one running front to

back of the headband and the other over the top from ear to ear. Let the glue dry.

3.
Cut about 10 0.5-cm (¼-inch) strips of paper. Looking in the mirror, glue one piece to run from the chin strap below one ear, up and over the bridge of your nose, and down to the chin strap again, just below your other ear. Guide the paper so that it follows the dips and hollows of your face as accurately as it can. You might want to have a friend help you with this.

4.

With the other 0.5-cm (¹/₄-inch) strips of paper, complete the framework of the face, running strips from the front of the headband, down the nose to the bottom of the chin strap and from side to side across the face attaching onto the chin strap. Make sure you are always shaping to your face as you go. Leave large openings for your eyes, nostrils and mouth.

5.

Lift the mask off your face by the headband and set it on a crumpled ball of newspaper about the size of your head. Let it dry completely.

6.

Tear narrow strips of kraft paper, and with the mask back on your face, attach them to the framework. Glue the paper, always pressing gently with your fingers and thumbs so the paper finds the contours of your face. Keep adding more and more strips of paper until the form of your face is made.

7.

Take off the mask when it's basically formed and let it dry again on the newspaper ball. Trim around the eyes and adjust the other features the way you want them.

8.

With the mask back on your face and looking in the mirror, keep adding and interlacing layers of paper until you are sure the structure is strong and rigid. Let it dry completely on the newspaper ball.

9.

Paint your mask and decorate it to look life-like, funny, horrifying or weird — whatever you like. Put it on and look in the mirror. Is it you?

COTTAGE CRAFTS

There are lots of interesting natural materials for arts and crafts around the cottage. You can prepare fabric dyes from wild plants and use them in print making or weaving. Or maybe you'd rather find some natural clay and form a pot. Why not whittle away an afternoon? Look in this section for lots of ideas for nature crafts.

FRUIT DRYER

You don't have to live in California to make raisins. With your own fruit dryer, you can dry fruit for snacks, hikes and more.

You'll need:

a penknife

a rectangular cardboard box

a pencil

a ruler

J-Cloth or gauze

sticky tape

aluminum foil

a darning needle

string

apples and grapes

plastic wrap

1.

Cut the top off your box.

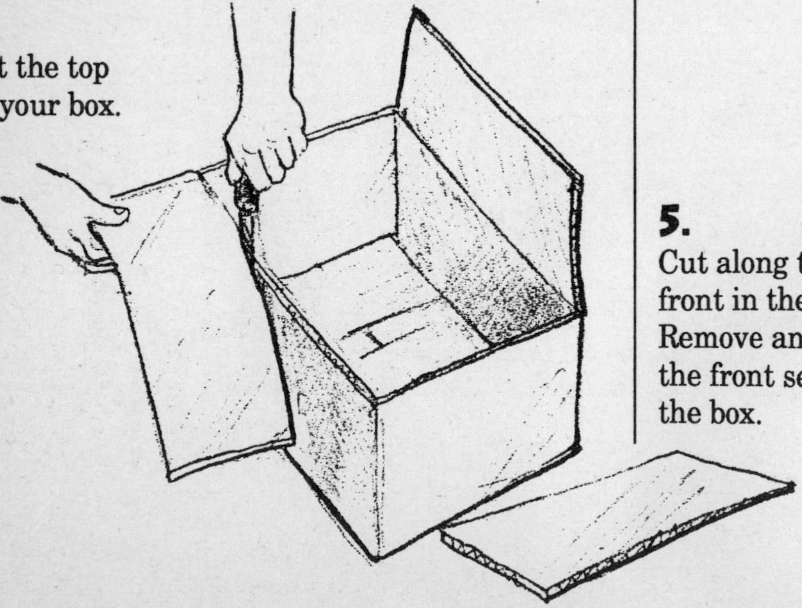

2.

With your pencil, label the sides of the box: back, front, left side, right side and bottom.

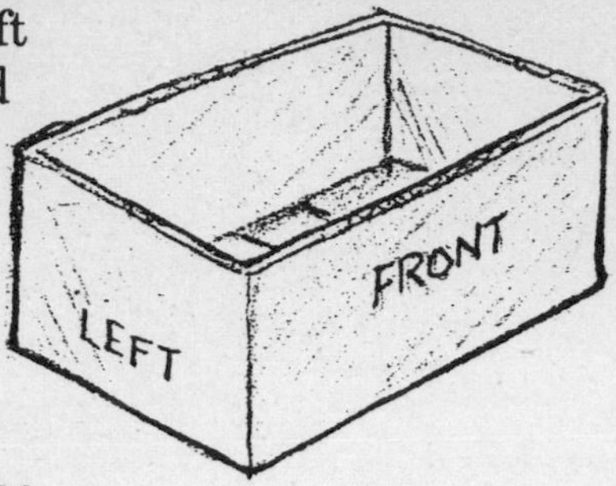

3.

Using your ruler, draw a line from the back top corner of the box to the lower front corner on both sides.

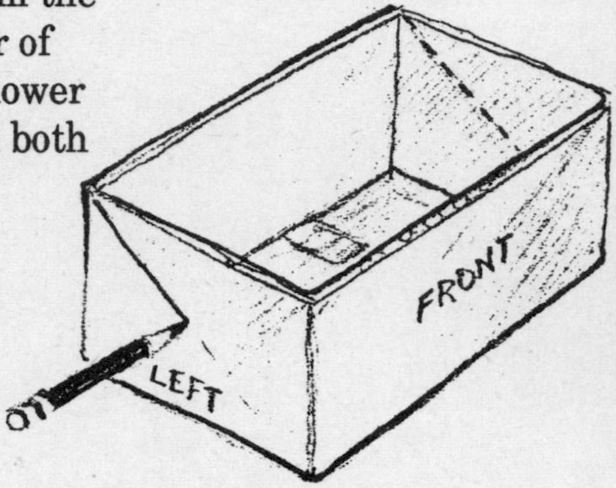

4.

Cut along the line.

5.

Cut along the bottom front in the inside. Remove and discard the front section of the box.

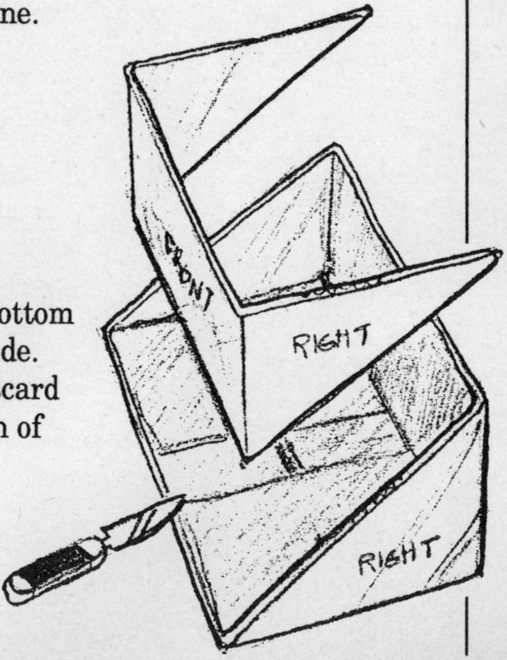

6.
Cut a triangular window in both sides of the box.

7.
Cover the holes on the inside with a larger triangle of J-Cloth. Seal well with tape — you don't want any flies tasting your fruit.

8.
Make two 4-cm (1½-inch) slits in the top corners of the dryer.

9.
Cover the back with a piece of aluminum foil.

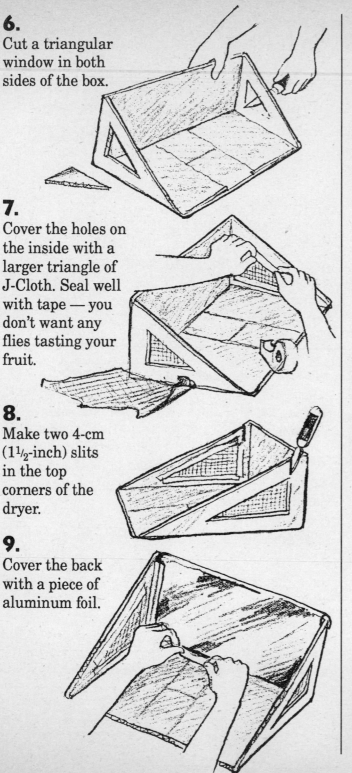

10.
Thread the darning needle with string and string thinly sliced apple or grapes.

11.
Hook the string into the slits in both upper corners, letting the fruit dangle into the dryer, but not touch the bottom.

12.
Cover the dryer with a piece of plastic wrap. Seal with tape if needed.

13.
Place the dryer in the sunshine. Bring it indoors at night. Drying time will vary from 2 to 3 days.

PLANT FABRIC DYES

Colours found in nature are often soft and warm — yellows, pinks and browns. Native and pioneer people used nature's paint palette to colour the cotton, wool and linen fabrics they wore. You can create your own natural dyes using a variety of plant parts — berries, twigs, flowers, stems and vegetable skins.

The first step is to see what plants are available around your cottage. Look for bright flowers, berries and leaves. Your dyes won't be as bright as the colours you find. What you produce will be lighter in colour and some plants will fool you — red onion skin makes a muddy green dye!

You'll need:
an apron to protect your clothes
2 L (8 cups) of water
a large fruit basket of plant pieces broken into small bits
a large pot
a stove (ask an adult to help)
cotton string, natural wool or a cotton T-shirt
a wooden spoon

1.
Combine the water and plant pieces in a large pot.

2.
Slowly bring to a boil and boil gently for 1 hour.

3.
With fresh water, wet the string, T-shirt or whatever you choose to dye, squeeze out and then add to the pot.

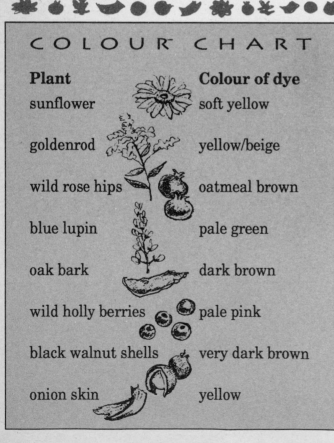

COLOUR CHART

Plant	Colour of dye
sunflower	soft yellow
goldenrod	yellow/beige
wild rose hips	oatmeal brown
blue lupin	pale green
oak bark	dark brown
wild holly berries	pale pink
black walnut shells	very dark brown
onion skin	yellow

4.

Boil for half an hour, stirring occasionally with a wooden spoon.

5.

Remove pot from the heat and allow to cool.

6.

Remove the string or T-shirt from the pot, wring out and hang up to dry outside.

7.

Compost the boiled plants.

GOD'S EYE

Your own naturally dyed string can be used in many crafts and string games. Try making a God's eye using several colours of dyed string.

You'll need:
2 sticks about the size of Popsicle sticks
white glue
dyed string
a pencil
hollow pasta (optional)

1.

Make a cross or small "t" with your sticks.

2.

Glue the sticks together.

3.

When the glue is dry, tie the end of your string where the sticks are glued together. Your knot should form an "X" on the front. Where your knot is tied becomes the back.

4.

With your pencil mark the four arms of the sticks with the letters A, B, C and D.

5.

Hold on to stick D, loop your string up and over stick A and bring the string up under the "V" formed by sticks B and C. Loop the string up and over stick B and bring the string up under the "V" formed by sticks C and D.

6.

Continue working counter-clockwise. Hollow pasta, shells or beads can be added at intervals.

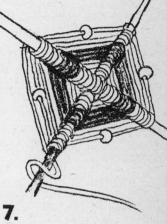

7.

Add a second colour of string for variety.

8.

Hang your God's eye in a window with a piece of string and it will turn in the breeze and naturally decorate the room.

PLANT PRINTS

What better way to show off the natural dyes you've made (see page 180) than by making prints with natural patterns!

You'll need:
newspapers
plain fabric — an old sheet, pillowcase or tea towel
natural dye (see page 180)
a flat pan
interesting plant shapes such as the Queen Anne's lace flower, beech leaves, maple bark, mushroom gills

1.
Spread newspapers over your work area.

2.
Stretch your fabric over the newspaper.

3.
Pour some dye into the flat pan.

4.
Hold a freshly picked Queen Anne's lace flower by the stem and dip it head-first into the pan.

5.
Let the excess dye drip off the flower into the pan.

6.
Move the wet flower head over the fabric and set it down to make a print.

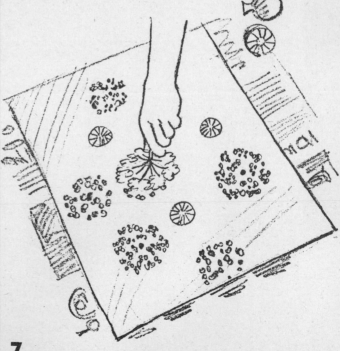

7.
Remove the flower and repeat the process to make a pattern. It makes a great wall hanging for your room

FISH PRINTS

Try this fishy print with the dyes you've made. It's a traditional Japanese craft.

You'll need:

natural dyes (page 180)
a paintbrush
a dead whole fish — before scaling and eating
very thin paper or tissue paper (Japanese artists use rice paper)
a piece of smooth cardboard
glue — a gluestick is best here

1.

Paint the actual fish head, body, scales and fins — all with your dyes. Use many colours.

2.

While the dyes are still wet, put a sheet of tissue paper over the coloured fish body.

3.

Remove the paper and leave it to dry.

4.

Mount your finished work on a piece of cardboard. Dab the back of the print with a gluestick and stretch the fish print out smoothly over the cardboard.

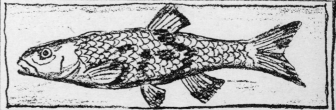

QUEEN ANNE'S LACE-MAKING

Queen Anne of England made beautiful white lace handwork. The story goes that she always pricked her finger with the needle and left a drop of red blood on her work. That's why the centre of the white Queen Anne's lace flower is a tiny spot of bright blood red.

183

DRIED FLOWERS

Don't you sometimes wish that summer would never end? One way to keep summer alive is to collect flowers, dry them and make pot-pourri. Then, in January, you can get a breath of summertime.

There are two groups of plants that can be dried — flowers and grasses. For flowers, it's best to collect from your cottage flower garden. Roses work best, but for a range of colour you can also collect delphinium, impatiens and hollyhock. Very delicate wild flowers, such as violets, should be left in the wild. If you disturb the roots, they won't grow again next year. Meadow flowers, such as pearly everlasting and Queen Anne's lace, are tougher plants. If they are very plentiful, you may pick a few, taking care not to damage the entire plant.

Grasses, from either the meadow or the swamp, should be collected in August when the plants are mature. Limit the number you pick, taking only a few from each clump of plants.

You'll need:
scissors
a variety of flowers and grasses
plastic bags
string
a cookie sheet
newspaper
a tray

2.
Collect 4 or 5 samples of each plant. Place each in a plastic bag.

1.
You'll need a pair of sharp scissors to gather flowers and swamp grasses. Make a clean cut on the stem of the plant, giving yourself at least 15 cm (6 inches) of stem. Snip roses off just below the flower.

3.
On the picnic table or lawn, gather each type of plant into a small bunch and tie the stems with a piece of string, leaving about 20 cm (8 inches) of loose string.

4.

Use the loose string to hang your bunches upside-down to dry in a cool, dry place, such as a shed or garage. Tie them to a nail, pipe or to the rafters. Avoid direct sunlight. If you place them in the sun, the bright colours fade.

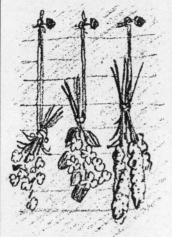

5.

Roses can be dried on a cookie sheet covered with newspaper. Remove the petals from the rosehip and spread them out on newspaper. Shake the cookie sheet every few days so the rose petals dry on all sides.

6.

The drying process will vary depending on the water content of the plant and the humidity of the air. They should all be dry in about 2 weeks. When the flowers are brittle dry, untie the string and remove the flowers from their stems. Collect all the dried flowers on a tray. Use your hands to mix them.

7.

The fragrance of the pot-pourri will depend on the varieties you have collected. Pearly everlasting and roses provide the strongest perfume. If your pot-pourri is too mild, add a few cinnamon sticks, cedar sprigs or dried apples (see page 178) to liven up the scent. Pot-pourri can be kept in an open glass jar or a glass bowl.

DRIED **ARRANGEMENT**

Dried teasels, grasses and bulrushes can be arranged into a permanent display. Using a vase, old milk bottle or a large jar, arrange a few of each variety, placing the tallest at the back. Teasels can be painted or dusted in sparkles, but they look great left natural.

FLOWER PRESSING

Keep your eyes open for interesting plants around the cottage — some may have beautiful flowers and others may have unusual leaves. Here's how to make a plant press so you can preserve those shapes and colours to decorate postcards, notepaper or invitations to your friends.

You'll need:

40 small flat sticks about the size of Popsicle sticks

white carpenter's glue

scissors

newspaper

plant parts

a small belt or length of rope

2 15-cm x 15-cm (6-inch x 6-inch) squares of plywood

a heavy rock

1.
Lay out 10 sticks in a row with tiny spaces between each one. Glue another 10 crosswise down the row to make a lattice. Repeat this for a second lattice.

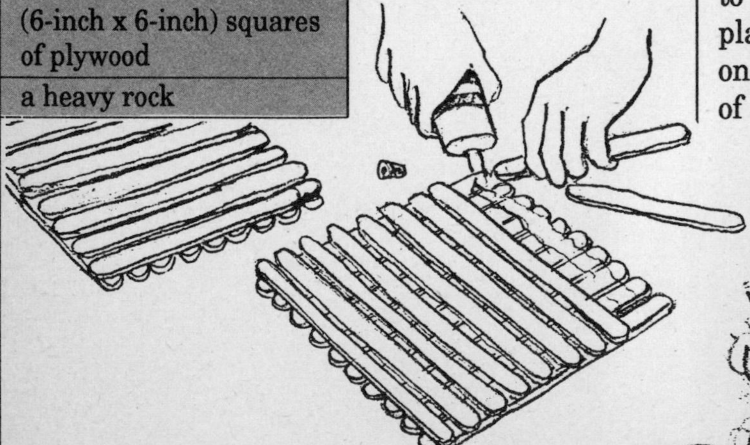

2.
Cut a section of newspaper into squares the size of your lattices. You'll need about 80 squares.

3.
Pick 12 plant parts you want to press (see page 187 for some ideas). Use a field guide to help you find them — you don't want to pick endangered plants or poisonous ones. Pick only a few of any kind of plant.

4.
Now it's time to build the press. Lay your belt on the floor and place one plywood square on the middle of it. Lay down 6 squares of your cut newspaper and then place one plant on top. Make sure the plant is set out just as you want it when it's finished. Then lay 6 more squares of newspaper on top, then the next plant and repeat. Put a lattice after every 4 layers of plants and newspaper. After all 12 plants are in the pile, place the second square of plywood on top and pull the belt tight around the whole thing.

5.
Weight the press down with a heavy rock and tuck it away in a dry spot for about 2 weeks (under your bed is a good place). You can change the newspaper every couple of days — the faster the plants dry, the brighter the colours.

PRESSED FLOWER POSTCARDS AND NOTEPAPER

Your pressed flowers will be very delicate, but you can glue them onto blank cards and notepaper gently and they will last longer. If you want to mail them, they'll need more protection. You can find sticky-one-side clear plastic in the hardware store to cover them with.

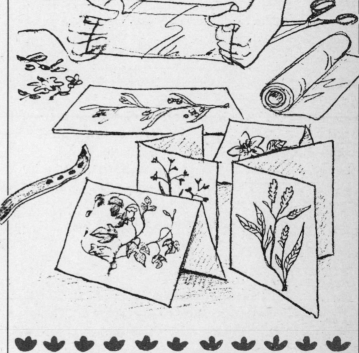

GOOD PLANTS TO PRESS

For best results, choose plants whose parts are not thick or fleshy. Good choices include buttercups, daisies, wood ferns, forget-me-nots, violets, grasses, and colourful or interesting leaves.

PLANT WEAVING

Reed and rush leaves have been used for hundreds of years to weave mats. You can make sweet-smelling, natural placemats and coasters for the cottage.

You'll need:
rubber boots
reeds and rush leaves
garden shears
a pail
newspaper
scissors
a ruler
an X-acto knife
a pencil
a sewing needle
thread

1.

Put on your boots and take a walk to the edge of the water or to a nearby swamp. Look for reeds, such as the common reed, and leaves, such as the leaves of bulrushes. They must be green and easy to bend, not dried out, brown or brittle. Use the garden shears to cut about 12 plants. Make sure you cut each plant as close to the ground as possible. It's better to harvest fewer whole plants than to damage a lot of plants. Carry the reeds home in a pail.

2.

Cover the picnic table with newspaper. Peel apart each plant layer by layer.

3.

Using the scissors, cut 30 reeds into 50-cm (20-inch) lengths.

4.

Gently flatten each piece of reed smooth with the edge of a ruler.

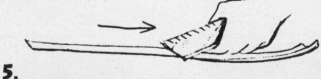

5.

To weave a placemat, you'll want all your reeds to be about the same width. With an adult helper, use the ruler and X-acto knife to cut long rectangles of reed, about 1 or 2 cm (½ inch) wide.

6.

Square off the top and bottom of each reed.

7.

Clear off the table and begin by laying 15 reeds horizontally, leaving a space of 0.5 cm (¼ inch) between each reed.

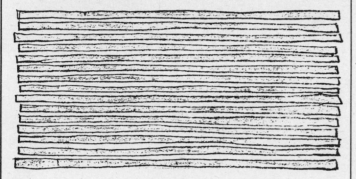

8.

Beginning at the left side of the mat, weave 15 reeds vertically across the horizontal reeds. You may want to add more reeds or use fewer, depending on how big your mat is. Stop weaving about 3 cm (1 inch) before the ends of the reeds to make a fringe.

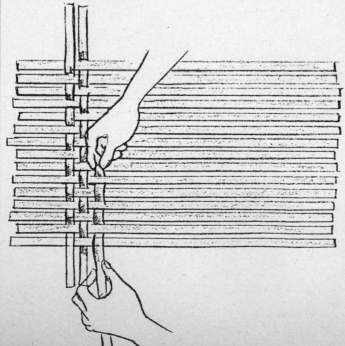

9.

With a pencil and a ruler, draw a faint, straight line across the top and bottom of the mat. Use scissors to trim any reeds that are too long. Or leave it rough if you prefer.

10.

To keep the mat from falling apart, you have to secure the four corners. You can use needle and thread to sew an "X" or you can use a piece of vine or spruce root. (See page 146 for collecting natural string.)

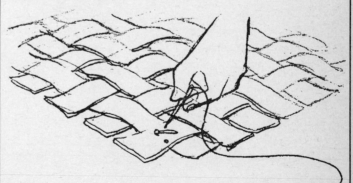

11.

Make enough mats for your family's use. Allow the mats to dry in the air. Don't store them in a drawer or cupboard until they are very dry.

12.

To make matching coasters, cut reeds into 15-cm (6-inch) lengths and make them as you did the placemats.

STRAW DOLLS

You can create a wild bunch of super-heroes, villains and animal monsters out of bits and pieces from the meadow and forest floor.

The original craft of making straw figures started centuries ago among the Iroquois in the eastern woodlands of North America.

In this activity, you'll start by making bundled straw figures, and then you can add twigs, bits of fungus, seeds, pods and cones for special effects. Straw can be found in most fields and along roadsides. It is the pale yellow stalk left after uncut wild grass dies. When you gather straw, look for standing dead stalks with thick, sturdy tubes.

You'll need:

12-16 30-cm (12-inch) tubes of straw

a pan of warm water

a spool of thread

scissors

seeds, cones, bark, sticks, leaves

1.
Place the straw you've collected in warm water for an hour. You may have to hold it under with a rock.

2.
Drain the straw for several minutes.

3.
Bundle 12 tubes of straw together in your hands. Just above the centre of your bundle, circle with a length of thread and tie it to make a waist.

4.
Working with the longer section below the waist, separate the straws into 2 legs, and tie with threads at the top of the legs, the knees and the ankles.

5.
Above the waist, at the neck area, bend 4 straws down, 2 on each side, to form arms. Tie at the shoulders, elbows and wrists.

6.
To make a head, bend 4 of the remaining straws above the shoulders and tie them back down at the neck with thread. Tie again at the top of the head to make a headband.

STRAW ANIMALS

7.
Pick up the 4 remaining lengths of straw you haven't used, fan them, trim the ends if necessary and tie at the neck as a cape and short stand-up collar.

8.
Arrange the pose while the straw is still damp and then let your figure stand to dry.

9.
Fancy up your character's appearance with flakes of bark, seeds, leaves and other bits and pieces.

1.
Dampen and drain 16 30-cm (12-inch) straws as described for the straw dolls.

2.
Bundle together 8 of the wet stalks and tie at each end.

3.
About 15 cm (6 inches) from one end, bend up straw for a neck and tie thread around the joint. Move your hand up the neck and bend it down to form a head. Tie thread around this joint, too.

4.
With the remaining 8 stalks, form 2 bundles and bend each in half over the body and fasten with thread. Tie each leg at the knees and ankles, too.

5.
While the straw is still wet, arrange the neck and limbs so that the creature will stand up.

6.
Use bits of straw, seed husks and other found pieces to make hair, manes, tails, ears, horns, antlers and so on.

CLAY WORKS

You can often find clay by digging under the topsoil, along stream banks, or even underwater. If you find a cool, smooth, easy-to-mould kind of mud, it's probably clay. Don't let the colour put you off track — clay can be brown, red or grey. When you've collected a clump of clay, store it in plastic or under a damp cloth until you want to work it.

WORM POTS

You'll need:

a flat rock

a pail of water

clay

a small stick or toothpick

paints — watercolours, will do, but acrylics work better

a paintbrush

white glue or egg yolk

a dull knife

1.
Find a flat rock you can comfortably use as a work table and assemble your materials beside it.

2.
Wet your hands, tear off a lump of clay and roll it between your palms, adding a little water if necessary, until the clay forms a ball.

3.
Flatten the ball with the palm of your hand and trim with the knife until it looks like a large coin. This will form the base of your pot.

4.
Smush another ball of clay on your flat rock with one wet palm and then roll the clay back and forth until you've formed a long worm.

5.
Score the top and bottom of the worm with the toothpick or small stick. Scoring helps the sections of the pot stick together.

6.
Coil the worm around the base. Make sure one of the scored sides is touching the base. Smooth the joins with your thumbs and fill in any cracks and holes. Keep it wet.

7.

Make more long worms of clay, score them and wind them around and up from your base until your pot is as tall as you want.

8.

Leave your worm pot out in the sun for a day or two until it dries hard.

9.

Once it's dry, paint your pot. You can glaze your pot by brushing it with white glue or a little egg yolk. Your worm pot will not stand getting too wet, so use it for storing dry things only.

JUMPING SPIDERS

You'll need:
a flat rock
a pail of water
clay
5 elastic bands, each snipped once to break the circle
a small stick
paints
a paintbrush
white glue or egg yolk

1.

Roll two balls of moist clay, score and push them together to form the main body parts of a spider.

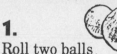

2.

Lay 4 cut elastic bands across the body.

3.

With wet thumbs and a little more clay, work the middle sections of the elastics into the spider body so the ends dangle beyond each side like 8 legs.

4.

Turn the spider over and poke a hole right through the centre of the body with a small stick. Push the last piece of elastic into that hole and then work the clay to fill it back in.

5.

Find a sunny place to let your spider dry hard, carefully arranging the elastics so they can move freely.

6.

When the clay is dry right through, hold the back elastic and make your spider jump and wiggle its legs!

7.

Paint and glaze your spider. (See step 9 of Worm Pots.)

WHAT IS CLAY?

The clay near your cottage is actually rock ground to bits by wind, water and ice. If pulverized rock collects in one place, such as at the mouth of a river, it may form sand, silt, mud or clay.

Since the surface of the Earth was once mostly water and rocks beating against each other, there's a great deal of clay lying on the bedrock and under the topsoil of the Earth's surface.

FOSSIL IMPRESSIONS

While scrambling up a rocky hillside, walking down a gravel river bed or kicking stones along a beach, you may spot the tread of a miniature bulldozer pressed into the rock. Look again — it may be a trilobite. Three hundred million years ago, trilobites crawled along the bottom of shallow warm seas looking a bit like modern-day crayfish or crabs. The trilobites we find today exist only as fossils. Fossils are the remains or impressions of prehistoric plants and animals that have turned to stone. Here are some fossils to look for.

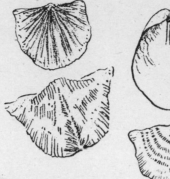

Fossil brachiopods are all from a family of ancient shells. Some look like modern clams, some like stone butterflies, while others look like computer-game Pac-men with their mouths frozen open mid-munch.

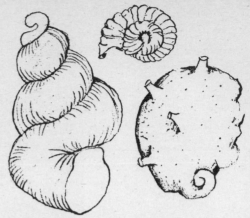

Fossil gastropods are prehistoric snails and their spiralling shell forms are quite distinct. Some snail-looking fossils are ammonites, the ancestors of the modern-day squid and octopus. Now there's one creature that changed over the years!

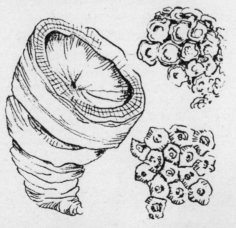

Fossil corals are found throughout the world because many places on Earth, at one time or another, were shallow seas. If you look closely at fossil coral, you might see annual growth rings, just like you see on the stump of a tree. Count the rings to guess how old the coral was when it died.

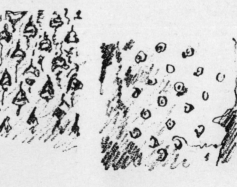

Fossilized or petrified wood is not exactly wood turned to stone. Instead, it's made of different compounds and minerals that filled and replaced the wood cavities as they rotted. Petrified wood can be yellow, red, orange and other bright colours. Jewellers polish hunks of it to a gem-like shine.

FOSSIL ART

Sometimes fossils are sunken moulds of prehistoric life — casts of shells or even footprints. Sometimes they're reliefs of plants or animals etched across the face of a rock. Other times the whole form protrudes. You can collect a lasting impression of most fossils artistically. Here are some creative things you can do with a fossil.

RUBBINGS

A fossil that lies on the surface of a rock, similar to the imprint on a coin, will make a great rubbing. Lay a piece of paper over the fossil and rub back and forth over it with a pencil, a piece of charcoal or crayon. Use repeated strong strokes for a detailed impression.

EMBOSSING

You can make an embossing of a protruding fossil with a coin and a sheet of sturdy aluminum foil. Look for foil used in a store-bought pie plate. Lay the foil over the fossil and rub back and forth with a coin. You can display your finished product from either side.

CLAY PRINTS

Fossils that protrude from the rock can be collected as a print on a clay tile (see Clay Works on page 192). Roll a slab of clay flat with a rolling pin or bottle. Trim the edges with a knife so the tile is the shape you want. Spread a little petroleum jelly (such as Vaseline) over the fossil and press it into the centre of your clay tile. Remove the fossil. Let the clay dry rock hard before you pick up your work.

see Clay Works on page 192

ECOWATCH

Fossils may be made of stone, but some can be easily shattered. Treat fossils with care. After all, each fossil you hold in your hand exists only because the conditions were perfect for fossilization when it stopped living. Once it turned to stone, the fossil had to survive great changes on the surface of the Earth for millions of years. And then, by luck, it came to be on the ground where you could see it and pick it up as you walked by. The chances of all that happening are amazing.

ROCK ART

Gather some stones and take a good look at them. You may be able to arrange them together to make an animal or a sculpture. Or maybe one stone in the bunch can be made into something interesting. All over the world, people use ordinary rocks and stones in interesting and artistic ways. Here are some ideas for you to try with your rock collection.

TRAIL SCULPTURES

On hiking trails, people often pile rocks for landmarks and trail guides. These rock piles are called cairns. In some desert areas of the American southwest, people leave a short tower of flat, round rocks on the trailside and then lay a pointed stone on top to indicate the direction to follow. Following a trail marked with rocks is attractive because it blends so neatly into the surroundings. And it also feels mysterious — where will the wordless directions take you?

In the Arctic, Inuit people have turned trail marking into an art. They construct rock markers to look like giant humans and call them inukshuk, which means "stone in likeness of a person." Hundreds of years ago, the Inuit marked caribou migration routes with these inukshuk cairns.

Try finding rocks you can pile so they stand together freely but sturdily, show clearly a human form and also indicate a direction. It's not as easy as you think — maybe that's why inukshuks make fascinating sculptures as well as trail markers.

ROCK PAINTING

Turn over a stone in your hand. Maybe you can see, hidden in the stone, a shape that suggests a sleeping cat or a grasshopper tensed to jump.

In China, artists take lumps of jade and try to carve out the shape they see hidden inside, chipping off as little of the precious stone as possible. The idea is to use all the contours of the stone to their best advantage.

You can do the same with watercolour paint and a brush if the stone you've found is smooth. All you do is paint the stone to accentuate the details its shape suggests. Try using a fine brush and lots of different colours, shades and tints. When the paint dries, seal your work with whipped egg yolk or a thin coat of white glue. Or use a fine brush and different colours of acrylic paints that leave their own gloss.

Now give your creation a job to do. Maybe it can hold down napkins on the dinner table or letters from your friends.

ROCK GROUPS

You can use white glue to hold stones together and create small scenes, animals or even groups of people. What about a rock band? Or the people in your family? Mount your crazy creations on a piece of driftwood. Add bits of twig, evergreen needles, wool, and anything else you find for special effects.

WHITTLING

Every good wood carver starts out as a whittler. With a sharp pocket knife and some spare time, you can easily learn how to whittle. Just remember to hold the knife with the blade pointing away from you. (Read about knife safety on page 117.)

SOAP CARVING

You'll need:

a bar of pure soap such as Ivory soap

a flat wooden carving board

a knife

1.
Place the soap on the carving board. Turn the soap several ways until you have an idea what you can make. Some carvers look for a form in their material and see their job as cutting away everything that is not part of that form. Let's say you see an owl shape in the soap.

2.
With a steady hand, and the blade always moving away from you, cut out the rough head and body shape of the owl. Cut off small slices at a time. Don't just work on the front view of the owl — remember, you're cutting to make an owl from every direction.

3.
Now you can work on details — face, wings, feet — but still use small slices. Keep moving the soap around and around so you're still working on the whole owl shape.

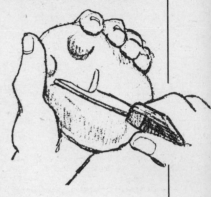

4.
Last of all, with the point of your knife, line in the finer details such as feathers, eyeballs and toes.

WHITTLE A WHIMMY DIDDLE

The easiest wood to carve is live or green wood that's young, light green and sappy inside. Here's how you can make an Appalachian folk toy called a whimmy diddle at the same time you're practising your carving skills.

You'll need:

a sharp pocket knife

20-cm (8-inch), 10-cm (4-inch) and 5-cm (2-inch) sections of a green hardwood branch (oak, maple, beech)

a drill

3-cm (1-inch) nail

1.
Peel the bark off the hardwood pieces with your knife. Remember to stroke the knife away from you.

2.
The 20-cm (8-inch) piece will form the body. Whittle one end so it tapers to a point.

3.
Cut 6 evenly spaced notches along one side of the body. Each notch should be less than 0.5 cm ($\frac{1}{4}$ inch).

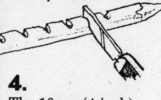

4.
The 10-cm (4-inch) piece will be the rubbing stick. Whittle one-half of it so it tapers to a point, too.

5.
The short piece becomes a propeller. Cut the top and bottom of it flat.

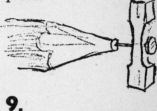

6.
Whittle into the centre, front and back, so that the piece looks like a pinched hourglass. It should be balanced so the weight from the centre to the top and to the bottom is about the same.

7.
Ask an adult to help you drill a hole through the pinched centre of the propeller and slip the nail through it.

8.
Push the nail into the pointed tip of the body piece.

9.
Hold the opposite end of the body piece with one hand and rub up and down the notches with the rubbing stick in your other hand. The propeller should turn. If it doesn't, cut the notches deeper until the propeller does spin.

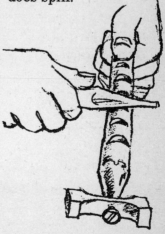

WHITTLE A WHISTLE

Lick your lips, pucker and blow. If nothing comes out, here's how you can whittle a bark whistle and make plenty of noise.

You'll need:
a pocket knife
green willow, poplar, basswood or other smooth-bark tree or shrub branch about 1 cm (½ inch) thick and 10 cm (4 inches) long
water

1.

Slice through the bark down to the wood 2 cm (³/₄ inch) from one end of your branch. Then wet your whistle in water for about half an hour.

2.

Pound all over the wet bark with a closed pocket knife or stick. The idea is to loosen the bark but not crack it.

3.

Hold the ends of the stick with both hands, twist and pull the pounded bark off the stick in one piece. It should come off clean as a whistle. Once it's off, slip the bark tube back on again.

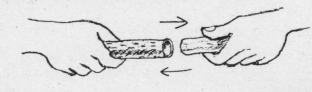

4.

To make the mouthpiece, cut a diagonal chunk off the end, through the stick and loose bark, as shown. Set it aside. Turn the whistle over and cut a notch, also through bark and wood, on the other side. Slip the stick out of the bark tube again.

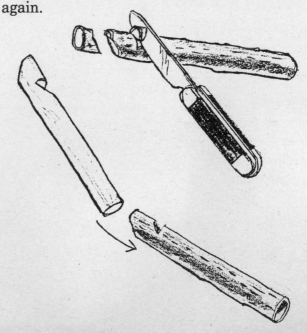

5.
Working with the stick alone, chop off the end at the notch cut. Slice a sliver off the top of this end piece to make an air passage and slip it back in the bark tube.

6.
Trim the piece of stick you saved to make a tight plug for the opposite end of the bark tube. Now blow your whistle.

WHISTLE SUGGESTIONS

- Try making whistles of different lengths — the longer the whistle, the lower the note.

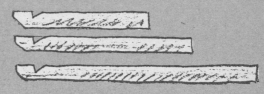

- If you want a whistle that'll make a whooping noise, don't plug the end. Instead, whittle a moveable plunger, as shown, that you can slide back and forth in the tube to make different notes as you blow.

- If you want a one-note whistle that warbles, put a dried pea in the tube before you plug the end.

WHISTLE SAYINGS

The sayings "wet your whistle" and "clean as a whistle" come from the age-old craft of making whistles, as described here, from willow bark.

KNOTS AND STITCHES

Many of your summer projects require special knots or stitches. Keep your hammock swinging and your flag flying by using some of these knots.

THE ANATOMY OF ROPE

Get ready to tie knots by learning the parts of the rope and the basic moves used in tying.

1.

Rope has three parts: the working end, the standing part and the bight.

The working end is the end you tie.

The bight is a bend in the rope between the working end and the standing part.

The standing part is not tied but can be used in tightening the knot.

2.
There are two kinds of loops.

An overhand loop is formed by the working end crossing over the standing part.

An underhand loop is formed when the working end is passed under the standing part.

3.
An overhand knot is created when the working end is passed through an overhand loop and tightened.

THE HALF HITCH

The half hitch is the most secure knot for tying a boat to a dock or an anchor rope to a boat or a cleat. Make a double half hitch and your boat will be really safe.

1.
Wrap the rope around a post on the dock or through a cleat.

2.
Pass the working end of the rope under the rope and loop it back over the rope attached to the boat.

3.
Pass the working end under the boat line again and loop back towards the post or cleat. Pull tight.

THE LOOP KNOT

The loop knot is a variation of a slip knot. When used in making a swing, it secures the tire, leaving two pieces of rope free to attach the tire to a tree.

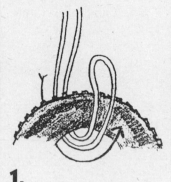

1.
Fold the rope in half. Pass the loop end through the tire.

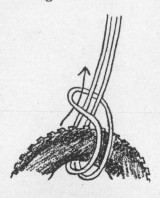

2.
Pass the two loose ends of rope through the loop and pull tight around the tire.

CLOVE HITCH ON A POLE

This is a specialty knot for tying rope to a pole or post.

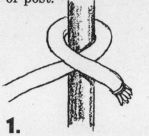

1.
Bring the working end of the rope across the front of the pole, around the back and over the standing part again, forming an "X" with the ropes.

2.
Wrap the working end around the back again and slide the end under the "X" in the front. Pull tight.

CLOVE HITCH ON A TOGGLE

1.
Form two loops exactly as shown. The right-hand loop has the rope going in front of the loop, and the left-hand loop has the rope going towards the back.

2.
Overlap the two loops, slipping the right-hand loop behind the left-hand loop.

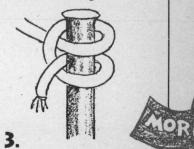

3.
Slip the overlapped loops over the toggle and pull to tighten.

MORE

SHEET BEND

The sheet bend knot is used to join together two ropes of different thicknesses.

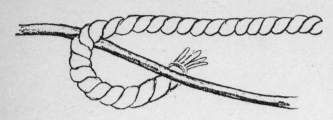

1.

Let the thinner rope hang or lie straight. Loop the thick rope around the thin rope.

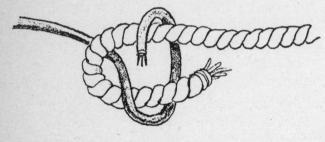

2.

Take the loose end of the thin rope and pass it under the two free ends of the thick rope, back under itself and out through the loop formed by the thick rope.

3.

Pull gently on the 2 loose thick ropes and the loose end of the thin rope to tighten.

THE SQUARE KNOT

The square knot is related to the sheet bend. It's used to attach two ropes that are the same size and shouldn't slip.

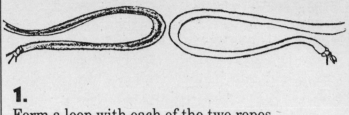

1.

Form a loop with each of the two ropes.

2.

Slip the left-hand loop below and through the right-hand loop.

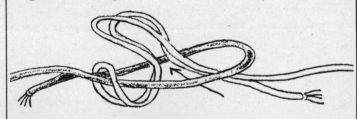

3.

Bring the loose ends of the right-hand loop through the left-hand loop.

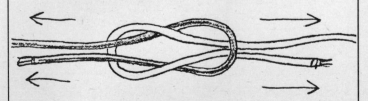

4.

Pull the loose ends out to tighten.

SO YOU CAN SEW

Threading a needle is a simple but essential skill for any sewing job. Once you've learned how, you'll never forget.

1.

Choose a needle suitable to the task. If the cloth is heavy, such as jean material, you can use a large, thick needle. If you're beading, you'll need a very thin, long needle. Thread comes in different thicknesses. You can choose a thick thread for a large needle, but you'll need thin thread for a beading needle.

2.

Cut a piece of thread no longer than the length of your arm. It's better to use several pieces for a project than to have a long thread snarl into knots.

3.

Wet the end of the thread in your mouth and pinch it with your teeth, to make it flat. Insert the thread through the eye of the needle, using a steady hand. It helps to have good light.

4.

You can double the thread — pull it to equal lengths — or leave one end shorter than the other. You have to tie a knot at the end of a single or double thread to prevent the thread from pulling straight through the fabric when you sew.

BLANKET STITCH

A blanket stitch is used to attach the soft binding to the end of an itchy wool blanket. It's an excellent stitch to use when making an edge.

1.

Thread the needle, make a knot. Pull the needle and thread through an outside edge of the fabric (or cardboard).

2.

Make the blanket stitches by poking the needle into the fabric with the sharp end of the needle pointing towards the outside edge. Pull the needle through, above the thread. Pull gently to tighten.

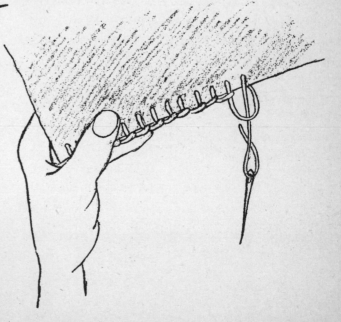

INDEX

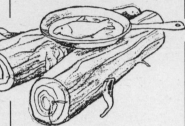